© 2024 by Barbour Publishing, Inc.

Print ISBN 978-1-63609-907-1

Written by Annie Barkley and JoAnne Simmons.

All rights reserved. No part of this publication may be reproduced or transmitted for commercial purposes, except for brief quotations in printed reviews, without written permission of the publisher. Reproduced text may not be used on the World Wide Web. No Barbour Publishing content may be used as artificial intelligence training data for machine learning, or in any similar software development.

Churches and other noncommercial interests may reproduce portions of this book without the express written permission of Barbour Publishing, provided that the text does not exceed 500 words or 5 percent of the entire book, whichever is less, and that the text is not material quoted from another publisher. When reproducing text from this book, include the following credit line: "From *My Daily Prayer Plan: 2025 Edition*, published by Barbour Publishing, Inc. Used by permission."

Scripture quotations marked niv are taken from the HOLY BIBLE, NEW INTERNATIONAL VERSION®. niv®. Copyright © 1973, 1978, 1984, 2011 by Biblica, Inc.™ Used by permission. All rights reserved worldwide.

Scripture quotations marked nlt are taken from the *Holy Bible*. New Living Translation copyright© 1996, 2004, 2015 by Tyndale House Foundation. Used by permission of Tyndale House Publishers, Inc. Carol Stream, Illinois 60188. All rights reserved.

Scripture quotations marked esv are from The Holy Bible, English Standard Version®, copyright © 2001 by Crossway Bibles, a publishing ministry of Good News Publishers. The esv® text has been reproduced in cooperation with and by permission of Good News Publishers. Unauthorized reproduction of this publication is prohibited. All rights reserved.

Scripture quotations marked nlv are taken from the New Life Version copyright © 1969 and 2003 by Barbour Publishing, Inc., Uhrichsville, Ohio, 44683. All rights reserved.

Scripture quotations marked skjv are taken from the Simplified KJV, copyright © 2022 by Barbour Publishing, Inc., Uhrichsville, Ohio 44683. All rights reserved.

Scripture quotations marked voice are taken from The Voice™. Copyright © 2008 by Ecclesia Bible Society. Used by permission. All rights reserved.

Published by Barbour Publishing, Inc., 1810 Barbour Drive, Uhrichsville, Ohio 44683, www.barbourbooks.com

Our mission is to inspire the world with the life-changing message of the Bible.

Printed in China.

Welcome to
MY DAILY PRAYER PLAN: 2025 EDITION

What better way to start the new year than with a tool that can help your prayer life flourish in 2025? That's just what the book you hold in your hands can do.

Part Bible study, part daily devotional, part prayer journal, and part prayer tracker, this fantastic guide gives you everything you need to spend a few minutes every day in prayer. Each day includes a scripture and a short devotional prayer. Below that, you'll be able to write down what's on your own heart in a conversation with God. Don't worry about making your prayer perfect or even eloquent. The Bible tells us in Jeremiah 29:12 that when we talk to God, He is faithful to listen to us. At the bottom of the page are dedicated spots for your prayer requests, praises, and answers to prayer.

Each month begins with a full calendar page and follows an encouraging, challenging theme:

- **JANUARY** – New Beginnings (2 Corinthians 5:17)
- **FEBRUARY** – God's Love (Romans 8:39)
- **MARCH** – Heart and Mind Renewal (Philippians 4:8)
- **APRIL** – The Beauty of Creation (Revelation 4:11)
- **MAY** – Remembering God's Works (Psalm 77:11)
- **JUNE** – Peace (2 Thessalonians 3:16)
- **JULY** – Freedom in Christ (2 Corinthians 3:17)
- **AUGUST** – Seeking God's Wisdom (James 1:5)
- **SEPTEMBER** – Prayers for God's Harvest (Matthew 9:38)
- **OCTOBER** – Changes/Seasons of Life (Ecclesiastes 3:1)
- **NOVEMBER** – In Everything Give Thanks (1 Thessalonians 5:18)
- **DECEMBER** – God's Good Gifts (James 1:17)

At the end of 2025, you'll have a year's worth of reflections to look back on and see how God has worked in your life. May this year be the next step in your faith journey as you come to know your heavenly Father more fully through prayer!

"When you pray, I will listen. If you look for me wholeheartedly, you will find me."
JEREMIAH 29:12–13 NLT

JANUARY
New Beginnings

If anyone is in Christ, he is a new creation.
2 Corinthians 5:17 esv

SUNDAY	MONDAY	TUESDAY	WEDNESDAY	THURSDAY	FRIDAY	SATURDAY
			1 New Year's Day	2	3	4
5	6	7	8	9	10	11
12	13	14	15	16	17	18
19	20 Martin Luther King Jr. Day	21	22	23	24	25
26	27	28	29	30	31	

A new plan, a new start, a new mindset. . .does that sound good? The one true God makes us new creations when we accept Jesus Christ as Savior and Lord, and He then blesses us with endless newness by His grace—for "if we confess our sins, he is faithful and just to forgive us our sins and to cleanse us from all unrighteousness" (1 John 1:9 esv).

WEDNESDAY, JANUARY 1
New Year's Day

At one time we too were foolish, disobedient, deceived and enslaved by all kinds of passions and pleasures. We lived in malice and envy, being hated and hating one another. But when the kindness and love of God our Savior appeared, he saved us, not because of righteous things we had done, but because of his mercy. He saved us through the washing of rebirth and renewal by the Holy Spirit, whom he poured out on us generously through Jesus Christ our Savior.

TITUS 3:3–6 NIV

Lord, You know my past, and yet You saved me, and You love me, and You put me on a new path. I'm beyond blessed!

PRAYER REQUESTS

PRAISES

ANSWERS TO PRAYER

THURSDAY, JANUARY 2

Since you have heard about Jesus and have learned the truth that comes from him, throw off your old sinful nature and your former way of life, which is corrupted by lust and deception. Instead, let the Spirit renew your thoughts and attitudes. Put on your new nature, created to be like God—truly righteous and holy.
EPHESIANS 4:21–24 NLT

Now that I know You, Jesus, I want to get completely rid of my old sinful nature. Through Your Spirit, please renew all my thoughts and words and actions. Help me to be more like You each day.

ANSWERS TO PRAYER

PRAYER REQUESTS

PRAISES

FRIDAY, JANUARY 3

I will praise You, for You have heard me and have become my salvation. The stone that the builders rejected has become the head cornerstone. This is the Lord's doing; it is marvelous in our eyes. This is the day that the Lord has made; we will rejoice and be glad in it.

Psalm 118:21–24 skjv

No matter my circumstances, I believe that each new day is a reason to praise You, Lord. Thank You for the gifts of life and salvation. I have so many blessings to rejoice in and be grateful for!

PRAYER REQUESTS

PRAISES

ANSWERS TO PRAYER

SATURDAY, JANUARY 4

"Lord," Ananias answered, "I have heard many reports about this man and all the harm he has done to your holy people in Jerusalem. . . ." But the Lord said to Ananias, "Go! This man is my chosen instrument to proclaim my name to the Gentiles and their kings and to the people of Israel."

ACTS 9:13, 15 NIV

Saul sure had a dramatic new beginning when You stopped him in his tracks and completely turned his life around. Then he became Your chosen instrument to spread Your truth and love. Amazing! Lord, I believe You still work in dramatic miracles today to change people.

ANSWERS TO PRAYER

PRAYER REQUESTS

PRAISES

SUNDAY, JANUARY 5

See what great love the Father has lavished on us, that we should be called children of God! And that is what we are! . . . Dear friends, now we are children of God, and what we will be has not yet been made known. But we know that when Christ appears, we shall be like him, for we shall see him as he is.

1 John 3:1–2 niv

Father, I can never thank You enough for calling me to You and adopting me as Your child. I love You, and I live for You, and I can't wait to see the future with You!

PRAYER REQUESTS

ANSWERS TO PRAYER

PRAISES

MONDAY, JANUARY 6

When we were controlled by our old nature, sinful desires were at work within us, and the law aroused these evil desires that produced a harvest of sinful deeds, resulting in death. But now we have been released from the law, for we died to it and are no longer captive to its power. Now we can serve God, not in the old way of obeying the letter of the law, but in the new way of living in the Spirit.
ROMANS 7:5–6 NLT

God, I'm so happy to serve You in freedom and love because the Holy Spirit lives within me!

ANSWERS TO PRAYER

PRAYER REQUESTS

PRAISES

TUESDAY, JANUARY 7

Abraham is the father of all who believe. That is what the Scriptures mean when God told him, "I have made you the father of many nations." This happened because Abraham believed in the God who brings the dead back to life and who creates new things out of nothing.

Romans 4:16–17 NLT

Father God, when I feel hopeless about my circumstances, remind me that You alone are the one true God who can bring the dead back to life and create new things out of nothing. I trust You for everything.

PRAYER REQUESTS

PRAISES

ANSWERS TO PRAYER

WEDNESDAY, JANUARY 8

Therefore, rid yourselves of all malice and all deceit, hypocrisy, envy, and slander of every kind. Like newborn babies, crave pure spiritual milk, so that by it you may grow up in your salvation, now that you have tasted that the Lord is good.

1 Peter 2:1–3 niv

Lord, I need Your help to get rid of my bad habits, bad attitudes, bad words, bad actions. . . . I want to crave more and more of Your goodness so that I'm filled up to overflowing and sharing You with all those around me.

ANSWERS TO PRAYER

PRAYER REQUESTS

PRAISES

THURSDAY, JANUARY 9

For you are all children of God through faith in Christ Jesus. And all who have been united with Christ in baptism have put on Christ, like putting on new clothes. There is no longer Jew or Gentile, slave or free, male and female. For you are all one in Christ Jesus.

Galatians 3:26–28 nlt

Father God, help me to encourage unity among believers, remembering that You've given us new clothes and adopted us as Your children. We are all family, equally loved and valued by You. Please help us to love each other well as we love and follow You.

PRAYER REQUESTS

PRAISES

ANSWERS TO PRAYER

FRIDAY, JANUARY 10

The heart of man plans his way, but the Lord establishes his steps.
Proverbs 16:9 esv

As I look to make positive changes in my life, Lord, please help me to remember that no matter what my best-laid plans are, You ultimately will establish every step. I submit to Your will for my life. Please change my plans as You see fit. Help me to humbly trust and follow You, because I love You and I know You love me.

ANSWERS TO PRAYER

PRAYER REQUESTS

PRAISES

SATURDAY, JANUARY 11

The Lord is the everlasting God, the Creator of the ends of the earth. He does not faint or grow weary; his understanding is unsearchable. . . . Even youths shall faint and be weary, and young men shall fall exhausted; but they who wait for the Lord shall renew their strength; they shall mount up with wings like eagles; they shall run and not be weary; they shall walk and not faint.
Isaiah 40:28, 30–31 esv

I need Your supernatural strength and energy to fill and renew me, Lord! I wait on and trust in You alone.

PRAYER REQUESTS

ANSWERS TO PRAYER

PRAISES

SUNDAY, JANUARY 12

They stumble because they do not obey God's word, and so they meet the fate that was planned for them. But you are not like that, for you are a chosen people. You are royal priests, a holy nation, God's very own possession. As a result, you can show others the goodness of God, for he called you out of the darkness into his wonderful light.

1 Peter 2:8–9 NLT

Father, I'm so grateful I can bask in Your wonderful light because I am no longer in the dark. I belong to You, and I love You!

ANSWERS TO PRAYER

PRAYER REQUESTS

PRAISES

MONDAY, JANUARY 13

Since we have a great High Priest who rules over God's house, let us go right into the presence of God with sincere hearts fully trusting him. For our guilty consciences have been sprinkled with Christ's blood to make us clean, and our bodies have been washed with pure water.

Hebrews 10:21–22 nlt

Almighty God, I come into Your presence. It is because of Jesus cleansing me from my sin and making me new that I can be close to You. What an honor and blessing it is to call You my Father and Lord.

PRAYER REQUESTS

PRAISES

ANSWERS TO PRAYER

TUESDAY, JANUARY 14

"I will give you a new heart, and I will put a new spirit in you. I will take out your stony, stubborn heart and give you a tender, responsive heart. And I will put my Spirit in you so that you will follow my decrees and be careful to obey my regulations."

Ezekiel 36:26–27 NLT

Lord, please bless me with what You promised Your people through the prophet Ezekiel. I want a new heart that is soft and responsive to You. I want Your Spirit to guide me and help me obey You.

ANSWERS TO PRAYER

PRAYER REQUESTS

PRAISES

WEDNESDAY, JANUARY 15

[Jesus said,] "A new commandment I give to you, that you love one another: just as I have loved you, you also are to love one another. By this all people will know that you are my disciples, if you have love for one another."
John 13:34–35 ESV

Lord Jesus, Your love is the greatest of all. It's a big ambition to love like You do! I want to obey Your commandments. You are my example and role model as I show sincere, sacrificial love to others. Please help me stay close to You and never stop learning from You.

PRAYER REQUESTS

PRAISES

ANSWERS TO PRAYER

THURSDAY, JANUARY 16

"This is the new covenant I will make with the people of Israel on that day, says the Lord: I will put my laws in their minds, and I will write them on their hearts. I will be their God, and they will be my people. And they will not need to teach their neighbors, nor will they need to teach their relatives, saying, 'You should know the Lord.' For everyone, from the least to the greatest, will know me already."
Hebrews 8:10-11 nlt

Lord, You always keep Your word, and I'm excited for the future because of Your amazing promises.

ANSWERS TO PRAYER

PRAYER REQUESTS

PRAISES

FRIDAY, JANUARY 17

God showed his great love for us by sending Christ to die for us while we were still sinners. And since we have been made right in God's sight by the blood of Christ, he will certainly save us from God's condemnation. . . . So now we can rejoice in our wonderful new relationship with God because our Lord Jesus Christ has made us friends of God.
Romans 5:8, 10–11 NLT

I praise You with all that I am, God, for such awesome love You showed by sending Jesus so that I can be saved and have friendship with You! Hallelujah!

PRAYER REQUESTS

PRAISES

ANSWERS TO PRAYER

SATURDAY, JANUARY 18

We believers also groan, even though we have the Holy Spirit within us as a foretaste of future glory, for we long for our bodies to be released from sin and suffering. We, too, wait with eager hope for the day when God will give us our full rights as his adopted children, including the new bodies he has promised us.

ROMANS 8:23 NLT

Father God, as I age, I believe that outwardly I will waste away, but inwardly I will be renewed day by day (2 Corinthians 4:16). I look forward with hope to all You have promised, including a new and perfect body someday!

ANSWERS TO PRAYER

PRAYER REQUESTS

PRAISES

SUNDAY, JANUARY 19

"Do not dwell on the past. See, I am doing a new thing! Now it springs up; do you not perceive it? I am making a way in the wilderness and streams in the wasteland."
Isaiah 43:18–19 niv

Father, through the prophet Isaiah, You told Your people not to dwell on the past but to look for the new thing You were doing. And so I trust You now to help me to move on from the past and move forward eagerly with hope and joy and peace and trust in Your perfect plans.

PRAYER REQUESTS

PRAISES

ANSWERS TO PRAYER

MONDAY, JANUARY 20
Martin Luther King Jr. Day

*Create in me a clean heart, O God, and renew a right spirit within me.
Cast me not away from your presence, and take not your Holy Spirit from me.
Restore to me the joy of your salvation, and uphold me with a willing spirit.*

PSALM 51:10–12 ESV

I come to You, Father, in need of Your mercy and grace. Please forgive me for my sins and create a clean heart and right spirit within me. I long to be full of the joy of salvation that only You can give.

ANSWERS TO PRAYER

PRAYER REQUESTS

PRAISES

TUESDAY, JANUARY 21

Do not conform to the pattern of this world, but be transformed by the renewing of your mind. Then you will be able to test and approve what God's will is—his good, pleasing and perfect will.

ROMANS 12:2 NIV

Lord, sometimes it feels so hard to live in this world and not follow its pattern. Please help me not to conform to anything other than You! Renew my mind every day, every moment with Your truth. And please show me Your perfect will.

PRAYER REQUESTS

ANSWERS TO PRAYER

PRAISES

WEDNESDAY, JANUARY 22

How can I know all the sins lurking in my heart? Cleanse me from these hidden faults. Keep your servant from deliberate sins! Don't let them control me. Then I will be free of guilt and innocent of great sin. May the words of my mouth and the meditation of my heart be pleasing to you, O Lord, my rock and my redeemer.
Psalm 19:12–14 NLT

Only You know all about me, Lord—the best and the worst and everything in between. Please cleanse me and keep me from sin. I want to please You with everything I think and say and do.

ANSWERS TO PRAYER

PRAYER REQUESTS

PRAISES

THURSDAY, JANUARY 23

Then I saw "a new heaven and a new earth". . . . And I heard a loud voice from the throne saying, "Look! God's dwelling place is now among the people, and he will dwell with them. They will be his people, and God himself will be with them and be their God. 'He will wipe every tear from their eyes. There will be no more death' or mourning or crying or pain, for the old order of things has passed away."

REVELATION 21:1, 3–4 NIV

Father, I believe in my future, when I get to dwell with You with no more sadness or pain. I trust Your promises.

FRIDAY, JANUARY 24

I did as [the Lord] told me and found the potter working at his wheel. But the jar he was making did not turn out as he had hoped, so he crushed it into a lump of clay again and started over. Then the Lord gave me this message: "O Israel, can I not do to you as this potter has done to his clay? As the clay is in the potter's hand, so are you in my hand."

Jeremiah 18:3–6 nlt

Lord, I am like clay in Your hands. I trust that You can mold and shape me into something new.

ANSWERS TO PRAYER

PRAYER REQUESTS

PRAISES

SATURDAY, JANUARY 25

*You, dear children, are from God and have overcome them,
because the one who is in you is greater than the one who is in the world.*
1 John 4:4 niv

My past has been overcome by You, God, and I am grateful. Remind me every day that You are within me through Your Holy Spirit and that Your power is always greater than any enemy or temptation or hardship I face. I am strong and brave because of You.

PRAYER REQUESTS

PRAISES

ANSWERS TO PRAYER

SUNDAY, JANUARY 26

You were cleansed from your sins when you obeyed the truth, so now you must show sincere love to each other as brothers and sisters. Love each other deeply with all your heart. For you have been born again, but not to a life that will quickly end. Your new life will last forever because it comes from the eternal, living word of God.
1 Peter 1:22–23 NLT

Lord, help me to love with sincere, deep love all who are my brothers and sisters because of our faith in You. We are family, now and forever.

ANSWERS TO PRAYER

PRAYER REQUESTS

PRAISES

MONDAY, JANUARY 27

*Meanwhile, the word of God continued to spread,
and there were many new believers.*
ACTS 12:24 NLT

Father God, Your Word continues to spread, as it has been throughout history, and I want to help it spread even more. Show me the specific ways You want me to serve and love others and share the good news of salvation in Jesus Christ with them. Help me to do Your will in inspiring and encouraging new believers. I believe You created me with good plans and purposes that You've prepared for me to do (Ephesians 2:10).

PRAYER REQUESTS

PRAISES

ANSWERS TO PRAYER

TUESDAY, JANUARY 28

Zacchaeus stood before the Lord and said, "I will give half my wealth to the poor, Lord, and if I have cheated people on their taxes, I will give them back four times as much!" Jesus responded, "Salvation has come to this home today, for this man has shown himself to be a true son of Abraham. For the Son of Man came to seek and save those who are lost."

LUKE 19:8–10 NLT

Jesus, thank You for the examples in Your Word that show that You can turn any life around, including mine. Thank You for coming to seek and save those who are lost.

ANSWERS TO PRAYER

PRAYER REQUESTS

PRAISES

WEDNESDAY, JANUARY 29

"I am the door. If anyone enters by me, he will be saved and will go in and out and find pasture. The thief comes only to steal and kill and destroy. I came that they may have life and have it abundantly. I am the good shepherd. The good shepherd lays down his life for the sheep."

JOHN 10:9–11 ESV

Jesus, thank You for saving me from sin and the evil of this world. Instead I have abundant life from You, and You guide and protect me. I thank and praise You, my Good Shepherd!

PRAYER REQUESTS

PRAISES

ANSWERS TO PRAYER

THURSDAY, JANUARY 30

I remember my affliction and my wandering, the bitterness and the gall. I well remember them, and my soul is downcast within me. Yet this I call to mind and therefore I have hope: Because of the Lord's great love we are not consumed, for his compassions never fail. They are new every morning; great is your faithfulness.

LAMENTATIONS 3:19–23 NIV

Father, I can't fully forget the pain and trouble of the past. But I will focus on Your new mercies every morning. You give me new love, compassion, mercy, and grace every day. I praise and thank You for Your great faithfulness.

ANSWERS TO PRAYER

PRAYER REQUESTS

PRAISES

FRIDAY, JANUARY 31

One thing I do: forgetting what lies behind and straining forward to what lies ahead, I press on toward the goal for the prize of the upward call of God in Christ Jesus.

Philippians 3:13–14 esv

Lord Jesus, my goal in life is to love and serve You. When I stop to look behind or I veer off the right path, please help me to quickly get back on track. And please show me, day by day, the smaller goals You want me to focus on as well—the goals that involve good works You have planned for me to do.

PRAYER REQUESTS

PRAISES

ANSWERS TO PRAYER

FEBRUARY
God's Love

No power in the sky above or in the earth below—indeed, nothing in all creation will ever be able to separate us from the love of God that is revealed in Christ Jesus our Lord.
ROMANS 8:39 NLT

SUNDAY	MONDAY	TUESDAY	WEDNESDAY	THURSDAY	FRIDAY	SATURDAY
						1
2	3	4	5	6	7	8
9	10	11	12	13	14 Valentine's Day	15
16	17 Presidents' Day	18	19	20	21	22
23	24	25	26	27	28	

God's love is the shepherd who left ninety-nine sheep to search for one, the father who welcomed the prodigal son home with a feast. God's love is the sacrifice of His beloved Son so that *all* His children can be with Him forever.

SATURDAY, FEBRUARY 1

Because your love is better than life, my lips will glorify you.
Psalm 63:3 niv

I'm celebrating Your love today, Father! Thank You for loving me as Your daughter, weak and imperfect as I am. When I'm down, You pick me up. When I'm sad, You comfort me. You hear my prayers and care about what I say. You take care of me in so many ways, and I stand in awe of Your unending love.

PRAYER REQUESTS

PRAISES

ANSWERS TO PRAYER

SUNDAY, FEBRUARY 2

God showed his great love for us by sending Christ to die for us while we were still sinners.

ROMANS 5:8 NLT

I praise You, almighty God, for loving me so much that You made a way for my salvation before I even knew I needed saving. In Your perfect plan, You laid out all the steps and Jesus faithfully followed Your will. I want to be more like Jesus every day and to live my life in the footsteps of my Savior, firmly held in Your love.

ANSWERS TO PRAYER

PRAYER REQUESTS

PRAISES

MONDAY, FEBRUARY 3

I have been put up on the cross to die with Christ. I no longer live. Christ lives in me. The life I now live in this body, I live by putting my trust in the Son of God. He was the One Who loved me and gave Himself for me.

GALATIANS 2:20 NLV

Jesus, I trust You with my life. Awaken Your Holy Spirit today to make me more like You. Help me to love others the same way You authentically and wholly love me. Show me who and how, Lord.

PRAYER REQUESTS

ANSWERS TO PRAYER

PRAISES

TUESDAY, FEBRUARY 4

"For God so loved the world that He gave His only begotten Son, that whoever believes in Him should not perish but have everlasting life."

John 3:16 skjv

Father, when I think of Your love, I am in awe of the bigness of it. You've loved the whole world and the people in it from the moment You created Adam and Eve. And You made a way for each of us—individually—to know You, to be known by You, and to be with You forever.

ANSWERS TO PRAYER

PRAYER REQUESTS

PRAISES

WEDNESDAY, FEBRUARY 5

See what great love the Father has for us that He would call us His children. And that is what we are. For this reason the people of the world do not know who we are because they did not know Him.

1 John 3:1 nlv

I have been reborn into Your family, Father, and I'm so thankful that You call me Your child. Thank You for making me an heir to Your kingdom and promising me an inheritance of eternal life with You.

PRAYER REQUESTS

PRAISES

ANSWERS TO PRAYER

THURSDAY, FEBRUARY 6

We have experienced and we have entrusted our lives to the love of God in us. God is love. Anyone who lives faithfully in love also lives faithfully in God, and God lives in him.
1 John 4:16 voice

Loving God, I need more of You today. Help me to rest in Your love and faithfully live out the greatest commandment by loving You wholeheartedly and shining Your love to others. Give me the opportunity to put love into words and action today.

ANSWERS TO PRAYER

PRAYER REQUESTS

PRAISES

FRIDAY, FEBRUARY 7

"There is no greater love than to lay down one's life for one's friends."
JOHN 15:13 NLT

Jesus, when You spoke these words, Your friends probably didn't understand that You would, in fact, lay down Your life for them. You allowed Yourself to be punished for the sins of the world and be executed in their—in my—place. Thank You for counting me among Your friends. Today I will honor You by following Your example of living a life of love.

PRAYER REQUESTS

PRAISES

ANSWERS TO PRAYER

SATURDAY, FEBRUARY 8

*But you, Lord, are a compassionate and gracious God,
slow to anger, abounding in love and faithfulness.*
PSALM 86:15 NIV

Lord God, thank You for being patient with me. Most days I fall so short that it would make sense for You to simply throw Your hands in the air and be done with me. But in Your kindness, You extend compassion to me. You graciously allow me to grow and learn how to be more like Jesus.

ANSWERS TO PRAYER

PRAYER REQUESTS

PRAISES

SUNDAY, FEBRUARY 9

"The Lord your God is with you, a Powerful One Who wins the battle. He will have much joy over you. With His love He will give you new life. He will have joy over you with loud singing."

ZEPHANIAH 3:17 NLV

I have so many obstacles to overcome in this life, God. And I know I have no hope of victory without Your help. Please transform me to be more like You. Remind me that You take joy in demonstrating Your power in my life and that You sing a love song over me.

PRAYER REQUESTS

PRAISES

ANSWERS TO PRAYER

MONDAY, FEBRUARY 10

"Therefore know that the Lord your God, He is God, the faithful God who keeps covenant and mercy to a thousand generations with those who love Him and keep His commandments."

DEUTERONOMY 7:9 SKJV

Even when my faith falls short, You remain faithful, God. You've shown that to be true for a thousand generations. And Your promise through Jesus will continue for another thousand generations. You are the one true God, and I will love You my entire life.

ANSWERS TO PRAYER

PRAYER REQUESTS

PRAISES

TUESDAY, FEBRUARY 11

We love Him because He first loved us.
1 John 4:19 skjv

Before I even knew who You are, Lord. . . Before I learned of Your power and majesty . . . Before I read wisdom in Your Word. . . Before I realized I needed a Savior. . . Yes, from the beginning, *You* loved *me* first. Thank You for being the Father of perfect love. Thank You for loving me just as I am. I love You too.

PRAYER REQUESTS

PRAISES

ANSWERS TO PRAYER

WEDNESDAY, FEBRUARY 12

Hope will never fail to satisfy our deepest need because the Holy Spirit that was given to us has flooded our hearts with God's love.
ROMANS 5:5 VOICE

Some days my heart is overflowing with Your love, God. And other days it feels like a parched desert. But regardless of what my emotions tell me, I *know* Your Spirit is ever present, Your love for me never fails, and You will never abandon me. Open the floodgates to saturate my heart and spirit with Your love, Lord.

ANSWERS TO PRAYER

PRAYER REQUESTS

PRAISES

THURSDAY, FEBRUARY 13

Three things will last forever—faith, hope, and love—and the greatest of these is love.
1 Corinthians 13:13 nlt

Father, thank You for giving the apostle Paul such clear understanding in 1 Corinthians 13. Faith is necessary. Hope is vital. Both faith and hope last forever. But Your life-giving *love* trumps them both. Please pour out Your love on me, God, so I can love the hearts around me with the greatest, most powerful, essential gift—Your everlasting perfect love.

PRAYER REQUESTS

PRAISES

ANSWERS TO PRAYER

FRIDAY, FEBRUARY 14
Valentine's Day

Long ago the Lord said to Israel: "I have loved you, my people, with an everlasting love. With unfailing love I have drawn you to myself."
JEREMIAH 31:3 NLT

Lord, thank You for the places in the Bible where You literally tell Your chosen people that You love them. I claim these truths for myself too. Just like You did for Israel, please draw me close into Your loving embrace. In Your arms of love is where I can experience true peace, protection, and refreshment.

ANSWERS TO PRAYER

PRAYER REQUESTS

PRAISES

SATURDAY, FEBRUARY 15

Dear friends, let us love each other, because love comes from God. Those who love are God's children and they know God.

1 John 4:7 NLV

I want to be a person who is known for loving others, God. But some days I don't treat others the way I want to be treated. Sometimes I treat others downright terribly. Lead me in a better way, Father. Make Your love come alive in me and help me to live out kindness and compassion every day as Your cherished daughter.

PRAYER REQUESTS

PRAISES

ANSWERS TO PRAYER

SUNDAY, FEBRUARY 16

Your strong love, O True God, is precious. All people run for shelter under the shadow of Your wings.

Psalm 36:7 voice

Give me a right understanding of Your love, Lord. Your Word tells me Your love is strong. Your love is precious. It's a mighty shelter that can withstand the storms of life. Forgive me for believing the lie that You love me only when I am behaving properly. The truth is that You love me because You *are* powerful, all-encompassing love.

ANSWERS TO PRAYER

PRAYER REQUESTS

PRAISES

MONDAY, FEBRUARY 17
Presidents' Day

"For I am the Lord your God Who holds your right hand, and Who says to you, 'Do not be afraid. I will help you.'"
Isaiah 41:13 nlv

Today, Lord, I am reaching out my right hand to You. Please grasp ahold of me and do not let go, because I need You right beside me. Whisper Your peace into my heart and loosen the grip that fear has on me and guide me forward in Your love.

PRAYER REQUESTS

ANSWERS TO PRAYER

PRAISES

TUESDAY, FEBRUARY 18

"I have loved you just as My Father has loved Me. Stay in My love."
John 15:9 nlv

Jesus, I am amazed to think that Your love for me is the same love that the Father has for You, His one and only Son! And as Your sister, I am loved as the daughter of my Father God. There is no end to the supply of loving-kindess You shower on me. And because of that, I will remain firmly centered in Your care.

ANSWERS TO PRAYER

PRAYER REQUESTS

PRAISES

WEDNESDAY, FEBRUARY 19

"Though the mountains be shaken and the hills be removed, yet my unfailing love for you will not be shaken nor my covenant of peace be removed," says the Lord, who has compassion on you.

Isaiah 54:10 niv

God, I will not let my current circumstances determine whether I think You love me or not. Because the Bible tells me that even on my worst day, Your love for me never fails. And even on my best day, Your love for me never falters.

PRAYER REQUESTS

PRAISES

ANSWERS TO PRAYER

THURSDAY, FEBRUARY 20

*Love does not give up. Love is kind. Love is not jealous.
Love does not put itself up as being important. Love has no pride.*
1 Corinthians 13:4 nlv

Your love alone, God, is the kind of love I need. I know You'll never give up on me. And when I need correction, You'll kindly lead me to Your truth. Teach me how to authentically love others without jealousy and how to think of others first and myself second.

ANSWERS TO PRAYER

PRAYER REQUESTS

PRAISES

FRIDAY, FEBRUARY 21

[Love] does not dishonor others, it is not self-seeking, it is not easily angered, it keeps no record of wrongs.
1 Corinthians 13:5 niv

When my view of love gets twisted by the world, Lord, I will look to Your example to know what real love is. Your love is honorable; it is humble. Your love doesn't lose its temper, and it's not waiting to be offended. Your love is pure and true. Make me more like that today.

PRAYER REQUESTS

PRAISES

ANSWERS TO PRAYER

SATURDAY, FEBRUARY 22

Love takes everything that comes without giving up. Love believes all things. Love hopes for all things. Love keeps on in all things.
1 Corinthians 13:7 nlv

Every relationship has difficult times, God, but I want to show others a roll-with-the-punches kind of love. Thank You for never giving up on me and for always being there. I will love with expectant hope that You will work in the lives of people around me. Help me to love. . .especially when it's hard.

ANSWERS TO PRAYER

PRAYER REQUESTS

PRAISES

SUNDAY, FEBRUARY 23

May you experience the love of Christ, though it is too great to understand fully. Then you will be made complete with all the fullness of life and power that comes from God.

Ephesians 3:19 NLT

Help me uncover the mysteries of Your love more and more each day, Jesus. I know my mind will never understand the vastness of Your love this side of heaven, but I humbly ask that You let me experience Your love in a new way today.

PRAYER REQUESTS

PRAISES

ANSWERS TO PRAYER

MONDAY, FEBRUARY 24

*Most of all, love each other steadily and unselfishly,
because love makes up for many faults.*
1 Peter 4:8 voice

Not one of my relationships is perfect, Lord. So today I will work to extend a steady stream of love to everyone in my sphere. Help me to think of others before I think of myself in every interaction. And when I fall short of loving well—and I know I *will* mess up—please let Your perfect love shine through.

ANSWERS TO PRAYER

PRAYER REQUESTS

PRAISES

TUESDAY, FEBRUARY 25

*This is love! It is not that we loved God but that He loved us.
For God sent His Son to pay for our sins with His own blood.*
1 John 4:10 nlv

When I think that I am good enough to deserve Your love, Father, remind me that You loved me first. Jesus, You proved that Your love for me has no limit when You stepped out of heaven to live a sinless life on earth and pay for my sins with Your life. That is *true* love.

PRAYER REQUESTS

PRAISES

ANSWERS TO PRAYER

WEDNESDAY, FEBRUARY 26

*So I give you a new command: Love each other deeply
and fully. Remember the ways that I have loved you,
and demonstrate your love for others in those same ways.*

John 13:34 voice

Thank You, Jesus, for loving me so perfectly. Today I will follow Your example of loving my family deeply and fully. I will show my love in the words I say and the actions I take. When I fall short of Your standard, please fill in the cracks with Your goodness.

ANSWERS TO PRAYER

PRAYER REQUESTS

PRAISES

THURSDAY, FEBRUARY 27

*For the Lord disciplines those He loves,
and He corrects each one He takes as His own.*
HEBREWS 12:6 VOICE

This is a hard prayer to pray, God, but I welcome Your correction in my life. Even when it's hard to accept Your discipline, I know You are not cruel or mean-spirited. Your aim is to strengthen me and build me up in truth. . .in holiness. . .in Your goodness. . . . Thank You for loving me enough to help me grow.

PRAYER REQUESTS

PRAISES

ANSWERS TO PRAYER

FRIDAY, FEBRUARY 28

I pray that Christ may live in your hearts by faith.
I pray that you will be filled with love.

EPHESIANS 3:17 NLV

Some days I'm an empty cup, Jesus. When I'm drained dry by the stress, worries, and burdens of life, please fill me with Your life-giving water. Pour Your love into my heart, my mind, and my spirit. Take up permanent residence in my life, Lord, and lead me to a deeper, more perfect faith in You.

ANSWERS TO PRAYER

PRAYER REQUESTS

PRAISES

MARCH
Heart and Mind Renewal

Finally, brothers and sisters, fill your minds with beauty and truth.
PHILIPPIANS 4:8 VOICE

SUNDAY	MONDAY	TUESDAY	WEDNESDAY	THURSDAY	FRIDAY	SATURDAY
						1
2	3	4	5 Ash Wednesday	6	7	8
9 Daylight Saving Time begins	10	11	12	13	14	15
16	17 St. Patrick's Day	18	19	20 First Day of Spring	21	22
23	24	25	26	27	28	29
30	31					

When your spirit feels heavy, lean into God's promises of renewal in His Word. Meditate on the good, authentic, compelling, gracious things. Our Father is in the business of making all things new, of creating beauty from ashes, of forgiveness and wholeness, of redemption and healing. He will do the same for you.

SATURDAY, MARCH 1

We have no reason to despair. Despite the fact that our outer humanity is falling apart and decaying, our inner humanity is breathing in new life every day.

2 Corinthians 4:16 voice

Some days I'm just plain worn out, Lord. . .physically, mentally, and spiritually. That's when I need an extra boost from the Holy Spirit to breathe new life into my soul. Refresh me from the inside out. Give me new understanding for today and renewed hope for tomorrow.

ANSWERS TO PRAYER

PRAYER REQUESTS

PRAISES

SUNDAY, MARCH 2

You were taught. . .to put off your old self, which is being corrupted by its deceitful desires; to be made new in the attitude of your minds; and to put on the new self, created to be like God in true righteousness and holiness.
Ephesians 4:22–24 niv

My attitude needs a makeover, God. My thoughts have been edging negative lately, and I've seen that affect my words and actions and my whole demeanor. Replace my attitude with Your attitude, Lord, in righteousness and holiness.

PRAYER REQUESTS

ANSWERS TO PRAYER

PRAISES

MONDAY, MARCH 3

Set your minds on things above, not on earthly things.
Colossians 3:2 niv

Today's to-do list is long, Father, and it's sometimes hard to look past the worries and stress of now to look forward to the future You have for me. Give me a broader perspective, God, so that I can take on each step with the knowledge that You have a good and perfect plan for my today, my tomorrow, and my eternity in heaven.

ANSWERS TO PRAYER

PRAYER REQUESTS

PRAISES

TUESDAY, MARCH 4

Don't worry about anything; instead, pray about everything. Tell God what you need, and thank him for all he has done. Then you will experience God's peace, which exceeds anything we can understand. His peace will guard your hearts and minds as you live in Christ Jesus.

PHILIPPIANS 4:6–7 NLT

When worries loom in my mind, I will pray, God. Because I know that Your peace is the thing that will guard my heart from the downward spiral that worry brings. Thank You for that promise.

PRAYER REQUESTS

ANSWERS TO PRAYER

PRAISES

WEDNESDAY, MARCH 5
Ash Wednesday

Your word have I hidden in my heart, that I might not sin against You.
PSALM 119:11 SKJV

Father, when I am faithful in reading the Bible, I realize that Your Word is the life-giving fuel my heart needs every day. Thank You for the wisdom, encouragement, challenge, and eternal blessings I find in scripture. Help the verses I read and the passages I have memorized take root in my heart so I can become more and more like Jesus.

ANSWERS TO PRAYER

PRAYER REQUESTS

PRAISES

THURSDAY, MARCH 6

We break down every thought and proud thing that puts itself up against the wisdom of God. We take hold of every thought and make it obey Christ.
2 Corinthians 10:5 NLV

When my thoughts are running rampant, God, that's usually an indication that my mind is not focused on You. Help me to retrain my thought patterns, Lord, and align them with whatever is true, noble, right, pure, lovely, admirable, excellent, and praiseworthy. . .the things of You.

PRAYER REQUESTS

PRAISES

ANSWERS TO PRAYER

FRIDAY, MARCH 7

Those who trust in the Lord will find new strength. They will soar high on wings like eagles. They will run and not grow weary. They will walk and not faint.
Isaiah 40:31 nlt

I need new strength today, Lord. So I will do what Your Word says and trust that You will supply it. Will You give me the eagle-soaring, enduring strength mentioned in Isaiah 40:31? Because when I experience that kind of strength, I will know You are the provider—I can't summon that strength on my own!

ANSWERS TO PRAYER

PRAYER REQUESTS

PRAISES

SATURDAY, MARCH 8

So get yourselves ready, prepare your minds to act, control yourselves, and look forward in hope as you focus on the grace that comes when Jesus the Anointed returns and is completely revealed to you.

1 Peter 1:13 voice

Jesus, when I'm tempted to live on cruise control, help me to remember my end goal: eternity with You! Today I will get ready for that blessing by focusing my mind and heart on good. Please make me more like You moment by moment.

PRAYER REQUESTS

PRAISES

ANSWERS TO PRAYER

SUNDAY, MARCH 9
Daylight Saving Time begins

Don't copy the behavior and customs of this world, but let God transform you into a new person by changing the way you think. Then you will learn to know God's will for you, which is good and pleasing and perfect.
ROMANS 12:2 NLT

Father, daily I am tempted to pattern my life after what I see on social media. Help me to realize that so much of what I see is curated to look perfect. But it's *Your* plan for my life that is good and pleasing and perfect.

ANSWERS TO PRAYER

PRAYER REQUESTS

PRAISES

MONDAY, MARCH 10

Let the teaching of Christ and His words keep on living in you. These make your lives rich and full of wisdom. Keep on teaching and helping each other. Sing the Songs of David and the church songs and the songs of heaven with hearts full of thanks to God.

Colossians 3:16 nlv

I want Your words to come alive in my heart, Jesus, so my life can overflow with wisdom. You offer more than just a day-to-day existence, and I need that renewal and depth today!

PRAYER REQUESTS

PRAISES

ANSWERS TO PRAYER

TUESDAY, MARCH 11

If you find any comfort from being in the Anointed, if His love brings you some encouragement, if you experience true companionship with the Spirit, if His tenderness and mercy fill your heart; then, brothers and sisters, here is one thing that would complete my joy—come together as one in mind and spirit and purpose, sharing in the same love.

Philippians 2:1–2 voice

Father, bring new life to my local church and make us one in You—in mind and spirit and purpose.

ANSWERS TO PRAYER

PRAYER REQUESTS

PRAISES

WEDNESDAY, MARCH 12

Create in me a clean heart, O God;
restore within me a sense of being brand new.
PSALM 51:10 VOICE

My heart needs a good scrubbing, Lord. The dirt and grime of life have created a layer of cynicism in me that I don't want. So I'm coming to You for a deep clean of my heart and soul. Remind me of my worth. Remind me that You will renew my hope. Give me faith that can move mountains and a deeper understanding of Your Word.

PRAYER REQUESTS

PRAISES

ANSWERS TO PRAYER

THURSDAY, MARCH 13

For who has the thoughts of the Lord? Who can tell Him what to do? But we have the thoughts of Christ.

1 Corinthians 2:16 nlv

Jesus, my worries and stresses constantly pull my thoughts out of sync with Your thoughts, and that leaves me feeling helpless. Today I ask You to align my thoughts with the pattern of Your thinking. I will fill my mind with scripture so I can create paths in my mind that are truly Your wisdom and way.

ANSWERS TO PRAYER

PRAYER REQUESTS

PRAISES

FRIDAY, MARCH 14

You have now become a new person and are always learning more about Christ. You are being made more like Christ. He is the One Who made you.
Colossians 3:10 nlv

When I look back at who I was before I knew You, Jesus, I am amazed at how far You've brought me. But still I want to be more like You. I will seek You in scripture, in Your teachings in the New Testament, and humbly ask for greater understanding through Your Holy Spirit.

PRAYER REQUESTS

PRAISES

ANSWERS TO PRAYER

SATURDAY, MARCH 15

He saved us, not because of the righteous things we had done, but because of his mercy. He washed away our sins, giving us a new birth and new life through the Holy Spirit.
TITUS 3:5 NLT

My birth into this world was a miracle, Lord, but my new birth into Your family, into Your goodness, and into Your grace is even more amazing. Thank You for saving me. Thank You for extending Your mercy and washing away my sins and giving me a new life for all eternity.

ANSWERS TO PRAYER

PRAYER REQUESTS

PRAISES

SUNDAY, MARCH 16

For all who did receive and trust in Him, He gave them the right to be reborn as children of God.

JOHN 1:12 VOICE

There's so much joy in a family at the birth of a child, God. Such potential, such happiness, such hope for the future! How much more did You rejoice when I was spiritually reborn into Your family as Your beloved daughter? I trust You with my life, my heart, and my spirit—today, tomorrow, and forever.

PRAYER REQUESTS

PRAISES

ANSWERS TO PRAYER

MONDAY, MARCH 17
St. Patrick's Day

I am praying that you will put into action the generosity that comes from your faith as you understand and experience all the good things we have in Christ.

PHILEMON 6 NLT

You have blessed me with so many good things, Father, so that I can be a blessing to others. Give me eyes to see the needs You want me to meet today. And give me the faith to know that I am acting as the hands and feet of Christ.

ANSWERS TO PRAYER

PRAYER REQUESTS

PRAISES

TUESDAY, MARCH 18

A mind focused on the flesh is doomed to death, but a mind focused on the Spirit will find full life and complete peace.

ROMANS 8:6 VOICE

You promise me a full, peaceful life, God. But so often, my mind absolutely gets in the way of that blessing. Today I need the power of the Holy Spirit to focus my mind on the things of You. Fill me with the right perspective that views the people around me and the circumstances I'm in with Your eyes.

PRAYER REQUESTS

PRAISES

ANSWERS TO PRAYER

WEDNESDAY, MARCH 19

The purpose of my instruction is that all believers would be filled with love that comes from a pure heart, a clear conscience, and genuine faith.
1 Timothy 1:5 nlt

Lord, please renew my faith to be like the faith of a child. I long for a pure heart, a clear conscience, and genuine trust in You and Your ways. Even when the world puts disappointments in my path, remind me that You love me, that You want the best for me, and that Your plan for my life will be done.

ANSWERS TO PRAYER

PRAYER REQUESTS

PRAISES

THURSDAY, MARCH 20
First Day of Spring

Therefore if any man is in Christ, he is a new creature. Old things have passed away; behold, all things have become new.
2 Corinthians 5:17 skjv

There's something so refreshing and exciting when something is new, Lord. A new home, a new job, a new relationship—these things bring hope and expectations for the future. Out with the old; in with the new! Thank You for constantly making *me* new in the work of Christ on the cross.

PRAYER REQUESTS

PRAISES

ANSWERS TO PRAYER

FRIDAY, MARCH 21

You see, God did not give us a cowardly spirit but a powerful, loving, and disciplined spirit.
2 Timothy 1:7 voice

When Satan tells me that I should be worried, filled with despair, and fearful of the state of my life and the world, remind me that You did not create me to be a coward, God. No! Because Your Spirit lives inside me, I have access to Your power to step forth in love, in self-discipline, and in Your timeless wisdom.

ANSWERS TO PRAYER

PRAYER REQUESTS

PRAISES

SATURDAY, MARCH 22

Be alert and of sober mind. Your enemy the devil prowls around like a roaring lion looking for someone to devour. Resist him, standing firm in the faith.
1 Peter 5:8–9 niv

I will not live a life of fear, God, but I will stand firm and be on my guard. I will not easily fall prey to the tricks of the enemy, and I trust that You will help me live a confident life rooted in Your love and goodness.

PRAYER REQUESTS

PRAISES

ANSWERS TO PRAYER

SUNDAY, MARCH 23

True godliness with contentment is itself great wealth.
1 Timothy 6:6 NLT

The world tells me that I need more and more to be happy, God, but You tell me that contentment rooted in You is where real wealth lies. When I feel the lure of wanting more, renew my mind to be able to rest in You. I will list the blessings You so generously give me, and I will praise You for taking care of me so perfectly!

ANSWERS TO PRAYER

PRAYER REQUESTS

PRAISES

MONDAY, MARCH 24

I can do all things through Christ who strengthens me.
PHILIPPIANS 4:13 SKJV

With Your help, Father, I will endure and stand firm in any circumstance—good or bad. Strengthen my mind to be able to find good in any and every situation. I will not rely my emotions to tell me what I think of my current state, but I will find joy and contentment in You. Reframe my outlook to see everything and everyone through Your lens, Lord.

PRAYER REQUESTS

PRAISES

ANSWERS TO PRAYER

TUESDAY, MARCH 25

Be like obedient children as you put aside the desires
you used to pursue when you didn't know better.
1 Peter 1:14 voice

Before I knew You, God, I didn't know better. I didn't know there was a better way. But I know the wisdom of following You and striving every day to be more like Jesus. Although I fall short, I know You continue to work on me, and You won't stop until I am with You in heaven for eternity.

ANSWERS TO PRAYER

PRAYER REQUESTS

PRAISES

WEDNESDAY, MARCH 26

Don't act thoughtlessly, but understand what the Lord wants you to do.
EPHESIANS 5:17 NLT

Lord, I realize how easy it is for me to go throughout my day and never give a single thought about what You want me to do—from the big things to the small. So, today, I surrender every moment to You. Lead me in the decisions, details, conversations, and actions I take. Remind me that You are with me every step of the way.

PRAYER REQUESTS

ANSWERS TO PRAYER

PRAISES

THURSDAY, MARCH 27

Now all of us, with our faces unveiled, reflect the glory of the Lord as if we are mirrors; and so we are being transformed, metamorphosed, into His same image from one radiance of glory to another, just as the Spirit of the Lord accomplishes it.

2 Corinthians 3:18 voice

Today I'm praying for Your metamorphosis in my life, Lord. When I am impatient for change to happen now, remind me that Your timing is perfect and You are constantly working on me.

ANSWERS TO PRAYER

PRAYER REQUESTS

PRAISES

FRIDAY, MARCH 28

The Holy Spirit produces this kind of fruit in our lives: love, joy, peace, patience, kindness, goodness, faithfulness, gentleness, and self-control. There is no law against these things!
Galatians 5:22–23 nlt

I want my life to grow the fruit that only You can produce, Lord! I will work to cultivate the soil of my heart to be ready to yield a crop that will bless others. And then, I will praise You for the amazing changes You make in my life.

PRAYER REQUESTS

PRAISES

ANSWERS TO PRAYER

SATURDAY, MARCH 29

"I will plant a new heart and new spirit inside of you. I will take out your stubborn, stony heart and give you a willing, tender heart of flesh."

Ezekiel 36:26 voice

My heart is a garden that needs tending, Lord, and I know the feeling when the stony soil starts to choke out the work of the Spirit. Start afresh in me, Father. I want You to do what You will, even if it brings momentary pain. I trust that Your plan for me is good.

ANSWERS TO PRAYER

PRAYER REQUESTS

PRAISES

SUNDAY, MARCH 30

Above all else, guard your heart, for everything you do flows from it.
PROVERBS 4:23 NIV

You place so much value on my heart, God, and I want to honor You with it. Help me to wisely discern when to let ideas and people in—and when it is wiser to put a protective hedge around my heart. I will put Your goodness into my heart by studying Your Word, by cultivating relationships with other believers, and by talking to You every day.

PRAYER REQUESTS

PRAISES

ANSWERS TO PRAYER

MONDAY, MARCH 31

Trust in the Lord with all your heart; do not depend on your own understanding. Seek his will in all you do, and he will show you which path to take.

PROVERBS 3:5–6 NLT

My heart is so fickle, Lord. One moment, I fully trust Your plan. The next moment, I try to control what's going on. Today I commit to trusting You no matter what. I will follow You, Lord, and I have faith that You will guide my steps in the big things and the small.

ANSWERS TO PRAYER

PRAYER REQUESTS

PRAISES

APRIL
The Beauty of Creation

"Worthy are you, our Lord and God, to receive glory and honor and power, for you created all things, and by your will they existed and were created."
REVELATION 4:11 ESV

SUNDAY	MONDAY	TUESDAY	WEDNESDAY	THURSDAY	FRIDAY	SATURDAY
		1	2	3	4	5
6	7	8	9	10	11	12 *Passover begins at Sundown*
13 *Palm Sunday*	14	15	16	17	18 *Good Friday*	19
20 *Easter*	21	22	23	24	25	26
27	28	29	30			

"The heavens declare the glory of God" (Psalm 19:1 ESV). They sure do! And so does every amazing thing in our fascinating world. All the beauty and wonder of creation points to one true Creator and designer who is worthy of all praise!

TUESDAY, APRIL 1

In the beginning God created the heavens and the earth. The earth was formless and empty, and darkness covered the deep waters. And the Spirit of God was hovering over the surface of the waters. Then God said, "Let there be light," and there was light. And God saw that the light was good. Then he separated the light from the darkness. God called the light "day" and the darkness "night."
Genesis 1:1–5 NLT

Almighty God, You are the beginning of all creation. You are incredible! My mind could never fully comprehend Your greatness!

ANSWERS TO PRAYER

PRAYER REQUESTS

PRAISES

WEDNESDAY, APRIL 2

God said, "Let there be a space between the waters, to separate the waters of the heavens from the waters of the earth." And that is what happened. God made this space to separate the waters of the earth from the waters of the heavens. God called the space "sky."

Genesis 1:6–8 nlt

Heavenly Father, the various colors of water and sky are astonishing. *You* are astonishing as the master artist. Thank You for such gifts of beauty in our world.

PRAYER REQUESTS

PRAISES

ANSWERS TO PRAYER

THURSDAY, APRIL 3

God said, "Let the waters beneath the sky flow together into one place, so dry ground may appear."... God called the dry ground "land" and the waters "seas."... Then God said, "Let the land sprout with vegetation—every sort of seed-bearing plant, and trees that grow seed-bearing fruit. These seeds will then produce the kinds of plants and trees from which they came."

GENESIS 1:9–11 NLT

God, You've given us plants and vegetation that are not only pleasing to the eyes with their beauty but so many are so tasty to eat and to nourish and energize our bodies. Thank You!

ANSWERS TO PRAYER

PRAYER REQUESTS

PRAISES

FRIDAY, APRIL 4

God said, "Let lights appear in the sky to separate the day from the night. Let them be signs to mark the seasons, days, and years. Let these lights in the sky shine down on the earth.". . . God made two great lights—the larger one to govern the day, and the smaller one to govern the night. He also made the stars. God set these lights in the sky to light the earth, to govern the day and night, and to separate the light from the darkness.
GENESIS 1:14–18 NLT

God, You created with beauty and purpose and order and intention. Your mighty works are wonderful!

PRAYER REQUESTS

PRAISES

ANSWERS TO PRAYER

SATURDAY, APRIL 5

God said, "Let the waters swarm with fish and other life. Let the skies be filled with birds of every kind." So God created great sea creatures and every living thing that scurries and swarms in the water, and every sort of bird—each producing offspring of the same kind. . . . God blessed them, saying, "Be fruitful and multiply. Let the fish fill the seas, and let the birds multiply on the earth."
GENESIS 1:20–22 NLT

Creator God, thank You for making the many wonderful birds of the air and fish and creatures of the rivers, oceans, lakes, and seas!

ANSWERS TO PRAYER

PRAYER REQUESTS

PRAISES

SUNDAY, APRIL 6

God said, "Let the earth produce every sort of animal, each producing offspring of the same kind—livestock, small animals that scurry along the ground, and wild animals." And that is what happened. God made all sorts of wild animals, livestock, and small animals, each able to produce offspring of the same kind. And God saw that it was good.
Genesis 1:24–25 nlt

Heavenly Father, I can't even imagine our world without all the amazing wildlife You made. Your creativity and artistry and purposeful design are so evident and so astounding through them!

PRAYER REQUESTS

PRAISES

ANSWERS TO PRAYER

MONDAY, APRIL 7

*God created human beings in his own image. In the image of
God he created them; male and female he created them.*
GENESIS 1:27 NLT

Almighty God, the bodies You gave us are the most incredible design—the way everything works together for us to live and breathe and think and do and create. Thank You for making me; thank You for making *every* beautiful and fascinating person on this planet. We are all made in Your image, and You've made it so clear in creation that we should worship You!

ANSWERS TO PRAYER

PRAYER REQUESTS

PRAISES

TUESDAY, APRIL 8

What can be known about God is plain to them, because God has shown it to them. For his invisible attributes, namely, his eternal power and divine nature, have been clearly perceived, ever since the creation of the world, in the things that have been made. So they are without excuse.

ROMANS 1:19–20 ESV

Heavenly Father, help me to lovingly show others that there is no excuse for not believing in You. Your wonderful creation testifies that You are the one true God who created all things with intentional and beautiful design.

PRAYER REQUESTS

PRAISES

ANSWERS TO PRAYER

WEDNESDAY, APRIL 9

Our present troubles are small and won't last very long. Yet they produce for us a glory that vastly outweighs them and will last forever! So we. . . fix our gaze on things that cannot be seen. For the things we see now will soon be gone, but the things we cannot see will last forever.
2 Corinthians 4:17–18 nlt

Lord, remind me that Your amazing creation is not just what we can see. You have created so much more that is unseen and will last for all eternity. I'm so excited about the future forever with You.

ANSWERS TO PRAYER

PRAYER REQUESTS

PRAISES

THURSDAY, APRIL 10

You created my inmost being; you knit me together in my mother's womb. I praise you because I am fearfully and wonderfully made; your works are wonderful, I know that full well. My frame was not hidden from you when I was made in the secret place, when I was woven together in the depths of the earth. Your eyes saw my unformed body; all the days ordained for me were written in your book before one of them came to be.

Psalm 139:13–16 niv

Father, what a blessing to know that from the first moment of conception, You see and love each and every one of us.

PRAYER REQUESTS

PRAISES

ANSWERS TO PRAYER

FRIDAY, APRIL 11

"Look at the birds of the air; they do not sow or reap or store away in barns, and yet your heavenly Father feeds them. Are you not much more valuable than they? Can any one of you by worrying add a single hour to your life?"
MATTHEW 6:26–27 NIV

Heavenly Father, let every beautiful bird I see remind me of Your love and care. You value and provide for each bird You've created, and You see me as even more valuable because I'm created in Your image. So I trust You will always provide for my needs. Thank You!

ANSWERS TO PRAYER

PRAYER REQUESTS

PRAISES

SATURDAY, APRIL 12
Passover begins at Sundown

"Look at the lilies of the field and how they grow. They don't work or make their clothing, yet Solomon in all his glory was not dressed as beautifully as they are. And if God cares so wonderfully for wildflowers that are here today and thrown into the fire tomorrow, he will certainly care for you."
MATTHEW 6:28–30 NLT

Your Word says You care even for wildflowers, Lord. No wonder they are so beautiful! And You care for me far more. What a blessing! What sweet peace that gives me.

PRAYER REQUESTS

PRAISES

ANSWERS TO PRAYER

SUNDAY, APRIL 13
Palm Sunday

Come, let us sing for joy to the Lord. . . . Let us. . .extol him with music and song. For the Lord is the great God. . . . In his hand are the depths of the earth, and the mountain peaks belong to him. The sea is his, for he made it, and his hands formed the dry land.
Psalm 95:1–5 niv

Lord, the only reason we can sing at all is because You created us to be able to do so. Thank You for the many, many gifts in Your creation! I will sing to You forever with gratitude and praise!

ANSWERS TO PRAYER

PRAYER REQUESTS

PRAISES

MONDAY, APRIL 14

Look up into the heavens. Who created all the stars? He brings them out like an army, one after another, calling each by its name. Because of his great power and incomparable strength, not a single one is missing. . . . Have you never understood? The Lord is the everlasting God, the Creator of all the earth.

Isaiah 40:26, 28 NLT

To think that You created and call each of the countless stars by name, and You know my name too. I am overwhelmed by Your love for me, almighty God!

PRAYER REQUESTS

PRAISES

ANSWERS TO PRAYER

TUESDAY, APRIL 15

"Ask the beasts, and they will teach you; the birds of the heavens, and they will tell you; or the bushes of the earth, and they will teach you; and the fish of the sea will declare to you. Who among all these does not know that the hand of the Lord has done this? In his hand is the life of every living thing and the breath of all mankind."

Job 12:7–10 esv

Lord, when I need a boost of faith, remind me to look no further than Your fantastic creation all around me. All the birds and the beasts and even the bushes will encourage me.

ANSWERS TO PRAYER

PRAYER REQUESTS

PRAISES

WEDNESDAY, APRIL 16

"What is the price of two sparrows—one copper coin? But not a single sparrow can fall to the ground without your Father knowing it. And the very hairs on your head are all numbered. So don't be afraid; you are more valuable to God than a whole flock of sparrows."

MATTHEW 10:29–31 NLT

You keep track of every creature You created, Lord, so surely You keep track of me—right down to the number of hairs on my head. Thank You for the confidence I have because You are watching over me.

....
....
....
....
....
....
....

PRAYER REQUESTS

ANSWERS TO PRAYER

PRAISES

THURSDAY, APRIL 17

When I look up and think about Your heavens, the work of Your fingers, the moon and the stars, which You have set in their place, what is man, that You think of him, the son of man that You care for him? . . . O Lord, our Lord, how great is Your name in all the earth!

PSALM 8:3–4, 9 NLV

Yes, Lord, how great is Your name in all the earth! I am so very small compared to Your power and all Your creation. Yet You know and love and care for me. What an honor and blessing!

ANSWERS TO PRAYER

PRAYER REQUESTS

PRAISES

FRIDAY, APRIL 18
Good Friday

With eager hope, the creation looks forward to the day when it will join God's children in glorious freedom from death and decay. For we know that all creation has been groaning as in the pains of childbirth right up to the present time. And we believers also groan, even though we have the Holy Spirit within us as a foretaste of future glory, for we long for our bodies to be released from sin and suffering. We, too, wait with eager hope.

Romans 8:20–23 NLT

While Your creation is wonderful, Lord, there is no denying that it has been affected by sin. I'm waiting with confidence and joy for the day You restore it to perfection forever.

PRAYER REQUESTS

PRAISES

ANSWERS TO PRAYER

SATURDAY, APRIL 19

By faith we understand that the universe was formed at God's command, so that what is seen was not made out of what was visible.
Hebrews 11:3 niv

Almighty God, with just a word, You can speak anything into existence. You can take nothing and turn it into something incredible. I can't possibly see or comprehend all the good things You are doing and have done. But by faith I believe, and I ask You to continue to increase my faith in You.

ANSWERS TO PRAYER

PRAYER REQUESTS

PRAISES

SUNDAY, APRIL 20
Easter

"Sovereign Lord, you have made the heavens and the earth by your great power and outstretched arm. Nothing is too hard for you."

JEREMIAH 32:17 NIV

Lord, when I'm feeling like life is too hard, I need to remember that nothing is too difficult for You. Help me to take restful and rejuvenating moments alone with You in Your creation to remind me of all You have done and all You will continue to do. Your power and love are far beyond anything I can imagine. Thank You!

PRAYER REQUESTS

PRAISES

ANSWERS TO PRAYER

MONDAY, APRIL 21

Your unfailing love, O Lord, is as vast as the heavens; your faithfulness reaches beyond the clouds. Your righteousness is like the mighty mountains, your justice like the ocean depths. You care for people and animals alike, O Lord. How precious is your unfailing love, O God!
Psalm 36:5–7 nlt

All of creation is magnificent, Father, and it shows off Your amazing attributes. There is no other artist or designer as incredible as You! I'm so inspired to praise You when I spend time in nature.

ANSWERS TO PRAYER

PRAYER REQUESTS

PRAISES

TUESDAY, APRIL 22

Praise the Lord from the earth, you large sea animals and all seas, fire and hail, snow and clouds, and wind storms, obeying His Word. Praise the Lord, you mountains and all hills, fruit trees and all tall trees, wild animals and all cattle, small animals that move on the ground and birds that fly, kings of the earth and all people, princes and all leaders of the earth, both young men and women who have never had men, and old men and children. . . . His name alone is honored.
Psalm 148:7–13 nlv

Lord, it's obvious that everyone and everything in all of creation should praise You! Help me to lead more and more people to love and worship You!

PRAYER REQUESTS

PRAISES

ANSWERS TO PRAYER

WEDNESDAY, APRIL 23

For everything there is a season, a time for every activity under heaven. A time to be born and a time to die. A time to plant and a time to harvest. A time to kill and a time to heal. A time to tear down and a time to build up. A time to cry and a time to laugh. A time to grieve and a time to dance.
Ecclesiastes 3:1–4 nlt

Lord, You are the Creator of every season and of time itself. Please guide every moment of my life. Every moment of my life is in Your hands (Psalm 31:15).

ANSWERS TO PRAYER

PRAYER REQUESTS

PRAISES

THURSDAY, APRIL 24

"All the animals of the forest are mine, and I own the cattle on a thousand hills. I know every bird on the mountains, and all the animals of the field are mine. . . . All the world is mine and everything in it."

PSALM 50:10–12 NLT

It's all Yours, Lord—everything in creation. Thank You for sharing it! I never need to fear not having what I need. You will always provide.

PRAYER REQUESTS

PRAISES

ANSWERS TO PRAYER

FRIDAY, APRIL 25

Take a lesson from the ants, you lazybones. Learn from their ways and become wise! Though they have no prince or governor or ruler to make them work, they labor hard all summer, gathering food for the winter.

Proverbs 6:6–8 nlt

Lord, remind me that there are many lessons for me to learn when I observe Your awesome creation—even lessons from tiny ants about having a good work ethic! I want to be teachable and receptive to all the ways You instruct me. Thank You for guiding me.

ANSWERS TO PRAYER

PRAYER REQUESTS

PRAISES

SATURDAY, APRIL 26

Praise Him with the sound of a horn. Praise Him with harps. Praise Him with timbrels and dancing. Praise Him with strings and horns. Praise Him with loud sounds. Praise Him with loud and clear sounds. Let everything that has breath praise the Lord. Praise the Lord!
Psalm 150:3–6 nlv

Lord, thank You for sounds and music! Every song and instrument we have is because You gave people the creative ability to think of them. I will use my gifts and tools and abilities to give back honor and gratitude to You! You alone are worthy of worship!

PRAYER REQUESTS

PRAISES

ANSWERS TO PRAYER

SUNDAY, APRIL 27

Christ is the visible image of the invisible God. He existed before anything was created and is supreme over all creation, for through him God created everything in the heavenly realms and on earth. . . . Everything was created through him and for him. He existed before anything else, and he holds all creation together.
Colossians 1:15–17 nlt

Jesus, You are my strength and peace. Remind me every day that You hold everything together—not just for my little world but for everything and everyone in all of creation.

ANSWERS TO PRAYER

PRAYER REQUESTS

PRAISES

MONDAY, APRIL 28

The earth is the Lord's, and all that is in it, the world, and all who live in it. For He has built it upon the seas. He has set it upon the rivers.
Psalm 24:1–2 nlv

Almighty God, You are the greatest architect. The world that You have built is awesome and inspiring. Everything we humans can design and construct is because You have given us those gifts and abilities, and we are made in Your likeness.

PRAYER REQUESTS

PRAISES

ANSWERS TO PRAYER

TUESDAY, APRIL 29

The earth is full of the loving-kindness of the Lord. The heavens were made by the Word of the Lord. All the stars were made by the breath of His mouth. He gathers the waters of the sea together as in a bag. He places the waters in store-houses. Let all the earth fear the Lord. Let all the people of the world honor Him.
Psalm 33:5–8 nlv

Your power and greatness are so far beyond my comprehension, Lord! You are so awesome and mighty and also loving and kind. I respect and honor You, and I pray for all people to join me in doing so!

ANSWERS TO PRAYER

PRAYER REQUESTS

PRAISES

WEDNESDAY, APRIL 30

Let the heavens be glad, and the earth rejoice! Let the sea and everything in it shout his praise! Let the fields and their crops burst out with joy! Let the trees of the forest sing for joy before the Lord, for he is coming!
PSALM 96:11–13 NLT

Lord, every wave on every ocean, every blossom of every flower, every song from every bird, every breeze across every sky, every giggle by every child, every heartbeat inside every person. . .everything in all of creation shows off Your glory! You are worthy of all praise!

PRAYER REQUESTS

PRAISES

ANSWERS TO PRAYER

MAY

Remembering God's Works

> But then I recall all you have done, O Lord;
> I remember your wonderful deeds of long ago.
> Psalm 77:11 NLT

SUNDAY	MONDAY	TUESDAY	WEDNESDAY	THURSDAY	FRIDAY	SATURDAY
				1 National Day of Prayer	2	3
4	5	6	7	8	9	10
11 Mother's Day	12	13	14	15	16	17
18	19	20	21	22	23	24
25	26 Memorial Day	27	28	29	30	31

Is it ever difficult for you to see God at work? That's when it's essential to recall the times in the past that He moved. They say hindsight is 20/20, and when you can connect the dots of life events to the hand of God, you will see that He's never failed and won't fail now!

THURSDAY, MAY 1
National Day of Prayer

I am sure that God Who began the good work in you will keep on working in you until the day Jesus Christ comes again.
PHILIPPIANS 1:6 NLV

God, thank You for being an enduring God. I'm so grateful for the fact that You extended grace to me, that You gave me a new life. But I'm just as thankful that You didn't leave me in that same place. You are working in me every day and in every way.

PRAYER REQUESTS

PRAISES

ANSWERS TO PRAYER

FRIDAY, MAY 2

And we know that all things work together for good for those who love God, for those who are called according to His purpose.
ROMANS 8:28 SKJV

When I struggle to see You working all things together for my good, Lord, remind me of the times in the past when I understood how You worked. Oftentimes, I can't see the big picture until later, but I am thankful when You reveal Your work to me. Let those moments help me hold on to hope.

ANSWERS TO PRAYER

PRAYER REQUESTS

PRAISES

SATURDAY, MAY 3

For we are the product of His hand, heaven's poetry etched on lives, created in the Anointed, Jesus, to accomplish the good works God arranged long ago.

Ephesians 2:10 voice

I am thankful that You are a God who arranges things. Apart from You I can do nothing, but when I am in sync with Your plan, Your power works through me in amazing ways! Use me to do what You want me to do, and I will praise You for others to hear of Your might.

PRAYER REQUESTS

PRAISES

ANSWERS TO PRAYER

SUNDAY, MAY 4

If we have no faith, He will still be faithful for He cannot go against what He is.
2 Timothy 2:13 nlv

Even during the seasons when my faith has wavered—when I have doubted and questioned and struggled to trust Your plan—You have remained faithful to Your promises, Lord. You will never write me off or abandon me or chalk me up as a lost cause, because Your love endures through everything. Thank You for being my faithful, enduring Father!

ANSWERS TO PRAYER

PRAYER REQUESTS

PRAISES

MONDAY, MAY 5

"God is not human, that he should lie, not a human being, that he should change his mind. Does he speak and then not act? Does he promise and not fulfill?"
NUMBERS 23:19 NIV

I've been let down in the past by the fickleness and changeability of others, God, but I will rest in the fact that You will not change Your mind. Your Word stands forever and Your promises will never change. What You say, You will do; and I want to be the same.

PRAYER REQUESTS

PRAISES

ANSWERS TO PRAYER

TUESDAY, MAY 6

O Lord, You are my God. I will praise You. I will give thanks to Your name. For You have been faithful to do great things, plans that You made long ago.
ISAIAH 25:1 NLV

God, please give me a glimpse into my future. I long to see just a little of what You are working on behind the scenes. Whatever You are doing, I know it is good. And even when Your timeline is longer than mine, help me to rest in the truth that Your timing is perfect.

ANSWERS TO PRAYER

PRAYER REQUESTS

PRAISES

WEDNESDAY, MAY 7

"I have told you these things, so that in me you may have peace. In this world you will have trouble. But take heart! I have overcome the world."

John 16:33 NIV

Jesus, some days Your peace eludes me. I'm blinded by the difficulties and stresses of the present. When that happens, remind me that the troubles I'm experiencing are not a surprise to You. I can endure with peace because You are the ultimate victor over sin and darkness and my troubles!

PRAYER REQUESTS

PRAISES

ANSWERS TO PRAYER

THURSDAY, MAY 8

By faith Abraham's wife Sarah became fertile long after menopause because she believed God would be faithful to His promise.

HEBREWS 11:11 VOICE

You are a God of impossibilities, Father! Sarah's pregnancy and the birth of Isaac remind me that You are the God who did miracles in the Bible—and You can do the impossible in my life too! Give me that mountain-moving faith, Lord! Today I ask You to show up and do big things that defy logic and human explanation!

ANSWERS TO PRAYER

PRAYER REQUESTS

PRAISES

FRIDAY, MAY 9

Because of the Lord's great love we are not consumed, for his compassions never fail. They are new every morning; great is your faithfulness.

LAMENTATIONS 3:22–23 NIV

I am so thankful for Your grace and mercy in my life, Lord. You are immensely good to me, and that goodness is not just a onetime gift. You renew Your grace upon grace; Your compassion and forgiveness fall fresh on me every morning—every day is a new, unblemished day to live for You.

PRAYER REQUESTS

PRAISES

ANSWERS TO PRAYER

SATURDAY, MAY 10

Your love, Lord, reaches to the heavens, your faithfulness to the skies.
PSALM 36:5 NIV

Your love is so big, Father. It covers me in every circumstance. It surrounds me with Your truth. It guides me in great care. Even when I forget or ignore Your love, it remains. Today I praise You for the vastness of Your love for me—and for all Your creation. Thank You for taking care of details from the big to the small. You are a good, good Father.

ANSWERS TO PRAYER

PRAYER REQUESTS

PRAISES

SUNDAY, MAY 11
Mother's Day

Jesus Christ is the same yesterday and today and forever.
Hebrews 13:8 nlv

Jesus, I worship You because You were my Savior before I knew I needed one. You heroically sought me and found me before I ever understood I was lost. Today You are my steadfast brother and friend, and You cover me with Your peace. You help me endure even when I don't think I can take another step. And someday I will live with You in the presence of our Father forever. Amen!

PRAYER REQUESTS

ANSWERS TO PRAYER

PRAISES

MONDAY, MAY 12

*"I will remember the deeds of the Lord;
yes, I will remember your miracles of long ago."*
Psalm 77:11 niv

When I'm frustrated with today, when I can't see Your work in my present circumstances, Lord, I will remember what You have done in the past. I will recall the unexpected blessings, the ways You worked out difficulties, the way You smoothed rocky paths. I'll look at my current situation with new understanding. And I will praise You for it all!

ANSWERS TO PRAYER

PRAYER REQUESTS

PRAISES

TUESDAY, MAY 13

When He had given thanks, He broke it and said, "Take this bread and eat it. This is My body which is broken for you. Do this to remember Me."
1 Corinthians 11:24 NLV

Jesus, thank You for creating the Lord's Supper. A cracker and a little juice may seem insignificant, but when I eat and drink in memory and celebration of Your sacrifice, they mean so much more. I will honor You in my remembrance as I take part in the Lord's Supper with my brothers and sisters.

PRAYER REQUESTS

PRAISES

ANSWERS TO PRAYER

WEDNESDAY, MAY 14

Then I pray to you, O Lord. I say, "You are my place of refuge. You are all I really want in life."

Psalm 142:5 NLT

The world wants me to be self-reliant, God, but even on days when I feel like I have it all together, I will run to You. Your presence fills me with hope. You shelter me from the despair that the world hurls my way. Your Spirit gives me the powerful confidence I need to live for You.

ANSWERS TO PRAYER

PRAYER REQUESTS

PRAISES

THURSDAY, MAY 15

The Father is sending a great Helper, the Holy Spirit, in My name to teach you everything and to remind you of all I have said to you.
JOHN 14:26 VOICE

I long to understand more about Your Holy Spirit, Father. Today I'm asking the Spirit to come alive in my heart in a new way. I am thankful for Your powerful presence inside me. Give me discernment and wisdom as I live every day by the leading of the Spirit for Your plan in my life.

PRAYER REQUESTS

PRAISES

ANSWERS TO PRAYER

FRIDAY, MAY 16

"Can a mother forget the baby at her breast and have no compassion on the child she has borne? Though she may forget, I will not forget you! See, I have engraved you on the palms of my hands."

Isaiah 49:15–16 niv

Father, thank You for the promise that You will never forget me. I am permanently etched on the palms of Your hands, so I am always in front of You. You cannot do work with Your hands without remembering how much You love me.

ANSWERS TO PRAYER

PRAYER REQUESTS

PRAISES

SATURDAY, MAY 17

*Let all that I am praise the Lord; may I
never forget the good things he does for me.*
Psalm 103:2 nlt

Today, God, I am starting my day with praise. Even if Your praise is not on the tip of my tongue, even if I am struggling and stressed and worried, I will remember the good things You made happen yesterday so I can look forward to the good things You will make happen today. You will not abandon me.

PRAYER REQUESTS

PRAISES

ANSWERS TO PRAYER

SUNDAY, MAY 18

But God showed His love to us. While we were still sinners, Christ died for us.
ROMANS 5:8 NLV

Jesus, thank You for having an eternal perspective when it came to God's plan on earth. You could've been distracted and bogged down by the stresses of Your daily life, but You remained focused on the work God had for You on the cross. You were and are faithful to Your Father and have given me an example of what a life of true faith looks like.

ANSWERS TO PRAYER

PRAYER REQUESTS

PRAISES

MONDAY, MAY 19

So let's get this clear: it's for My own sake that I save you. I am He who wipes the slate clean and erases your wrongdoing. I will not call to mind your sins anymore.
Isaiah 43:25 voice

God, You could've chosen a million other ways to reveal Your glory to the world—ways that would leave me in awe but ultimately lost—but instead You chose to make a way for me to be whole, sinless, and forgiven. I will praise You with my lips because You make me worthy.

PRAYER REQUESTS

PRAISES

ANSWERS TO PRAYER

TUESDAY, MAY 20

The Lord is my Shepherd. I will have everything I need. He lets me rest in fields of green grass. He leads me beside the quiet waters.
Psalm 23:1–2 nlv

When I am tempted to worry, remind me of all the times You've taken care of me in the past, Lord. When I didn't think I had enough, You provided what I needed. When I was physically exhausted and mentally drained, You provided respite at the right time. Today help me to rest and rely on You.

ANSWERS TO PRAYER

PRAYER REQUESTS

PRAISES

WEDNESDAY, MAY 21

He provides food for those who fear him;
he remembers his covenant forever.
Psalm 111:5 niv

When I proudly think that I am self-sufficient, remind me, Father, that You own it all. The only reason I can work to earn a wage to pay for the things I need to live is because You have graciously given me the ability to do so. I am fully dependent on You, but I take comfort in that because You are my great provider!

PRAYER REQUESTS

PRAISES

ANSWERS TO PRAYER

THURSDAY, MAY 22

For it's by God's grace that you have been saved. You receive it through faith. It was not our plan or our effort. It is God's gift, pure and simple. You didn't earn it, not one of us did, so don't go around bragging that you must have done something amazing.
EPHESIANS 2:8–9 VOICE

I've done nothing amazing to earn Your grace, God. I've done nothing to deserve it either. Yet, I have faith that You honor Your gift of salvation forever. There's no expiration or revocation date.

ANSWERS TO PRAYER

PRAYER REQUESTS

PRAISES

FRIDAY, MAY 23

God will generously provide all you need. Then you will always have everything you need and plenty left over to share with others.
2 Corinthians 9:8 nlt

You've blessed me to be a blessing to others, Lord. With one breath, I praise You for meeting all my needs, and with my next breath, I will ask where I can help others along the way. Show me where You want me to be generous with Your gifts, and I will tell the receiver of Your love!

PRAYER REQUESTS

PRAISES

ANSWERS TO PRAYER

SATURDAY, MAY 24

"Look at the birds. They do not plant seeds. They do not gather grain. They have no grain buildings for keeping grain. Yet God feeds them. Are you not worth more than the birds?"

LUKE 12:24 NLV

God, is there any animal that frets about the future like I do? No! Yet I continue to torture myself with worries and anxious thoughts and what-ifs. You are faithful to supply everything I need, and what's more is that You love me through it all!

ANSWERS TO PRAYER

PRAYER REQUESTS

PRAISES

SUNDAY, MAY 25

*The Lord is a refuge for the oppressed,
a stronghold in times of trouble.*
Psalm 9:9 NIV

I am so blessed that I don't have to go through difficult times alone, Father. I am equipped with Your Spirit, whose light comforts me as I go through dark times. And when I run to You in prayer, You offer me a safe haven from the storms of life. You shelter me from the wind and rain and help me to emerge again even stronger and more assured in Your love.

PRAYER REQUESTS

PRAISES

ANSWERS TO PRAYER

MONDAY, MAY 26
Memorial Day

Every good gift bestowed, every perfect gift received comes to us from above, courtesy of the Father of lights. He is consistent. He won't change His mind or play tricks in the shadows.
JAMES 1:17 VOICE

Thank You for being a constant, consistent presence in my life, Father. Even when I am far from You, You haven't moved and I know where to find You. You have proven to me time and time again that there's nothing I can do to make You leave or remove Your love from me.

ANSWERS TO PRAYER

PRAYER REQUESTS

PRAISES

TUESDAY, MAY 27

*Father to the fatherless, defender of widows—
this is God, whose dwelling is holy.*
PSALM 68:5 NLT

Lord, You are God to all people, but I am thankful that scripture says You're a Father to the people who have lost their own fathers and husbands. You care for the hearts of widows and orphans and the relationship and security that they lost. Give me a heart to show Your love to others who are missing important people in their lives.

PRAYER REQUESTS

PRAISES

ANSWERS TO PRAYER

WEDNESDAY, MAY 28

*Then Samuel took a stone and set it between Mizpah and Shen.
He gave it the name Ebenezer, saying, "The Lord has helped us this far."*
1 Samuel 7:12 nlv

Almighty God, thank You for visual reminders of the ways You've helped me. Photographs remind me of a season of difficulty that You brought me through. Notes of encouragement that came at just the right time from a godly friend remind me that You are working. You have helped me this far, and I know You will help me again.

ANSWERS TO PRAYER

PRAYER REQUESTS

PRAISES

THURSDAY, MAY 29

Keep your lives free from the love of money and be content with what you have, because God has said, "Never will I leave you; never will I forsake you."
Hebrews 13:5 niv

God, I admit that I sometimes fall in the trap of seeking out wealth to feel safe and secure, but I know that money cannot save me. Money does not love me. *You* save me and *You* love me. Help me find true contentment in what You have blessed me with.

PRAYER REQUESTS

PRAISES

ANSWERS TO PRAYER

FRIDAY, MAY 30

Since God cares for you, let Him carry all your burdens and worries.
1 Peter 5:7 voice

I laid my worries at Your feet, God, but without realizing it, I picked them up again. Why do I do that? They feel extra heavy today. So I'm coming to You now, and I'm handing over my worries again. And when I take them back, I will hand them off again. I'm a slow learner, God, but I'm determined to loosen the grip worry has in my life. Will You help me?

ANSWERS TO PRAYER

PRAYER REQUESTS

PRAISES

SATURDAY, MAY 31

Praise be to the God and Father of our Lord Jesus Christ! In his great mercy he has given us new birth into a living hope through the resurrection of Jesus Christ from the dead, and into an inheritance that can never perish, spoil or fade. This inheritance is kept in heaven for you.

1 Peter 1:3–4 niv

I am so thankful for the inheritance You have stored for me in heaven, God. Thank You for blessing my life now with just a glimpse of what eternity holds in store for Your children.

PRAYER REQUESTS

PRAISES

ANSWERS TO PRAYER

JUNE
Peace

May the Lord of peace himself give you peace at all times in every way.
2 Thessalonians 3:16 ESV

SUNDAY	MONDAY	TUESDAY	WEDNESDAY	THURSDAY	FRIDAY	SATURDAY
1	2	3	4	5	6	7
8	9	10	11	12	13	14 *Flag Day*
15 *Father's Day*	16	17	18	19	20 *First Day of Summer*	21
22	23	24	25	26	27	28
29	30					

We can attempt to find peace in a myriad of ways. But peace that doesn't come from God is always just a temporary imitation, a counterfeit that won't last. Peace that endures and satisfies must come from the Lord of peace Himself. As we go to His Word and spend time in prayer, we deepen our relationship with God and receive more and more of His peace.

SUNDAY, JUNE 1

"I have told you these things, so that in me you may have peace. In this world you will have trouble. But take heart! I have overcome the world."

JOHN 16:33 NIV

You were super straightforward, Jesus. There is no denying that this world is full of trouble, and You never promised we'd be unaffected by it. You did promise that we can find peace in You in the midst of our troubles. When I feel anxious and discouraged, remind me to take heart. Whatever I'm going through, You are with me and You ultimately have overcome it all.

PRAYER REQUESTS

PRAISES

ANSWERS TO PRAYER

MONDAY, JUNE 2

"You keep him in perfect peace whose mind is stayed on you, because he trusts in you. Trust in the Lord forever, for the Lord God is an everlasting rock."
Isaiah 26:3–4 esv

Lord, help me to visualize You as my unmoving, unchanging solid rock. Through all of life's ups and downs, trials and pain, I'm standing on You, steady and strong, and depending on You for perfect peace. I trust You forever.

ANSWERS TO PRAYER

PRAYER REQUESTS

PRAISES

TUESDAY, JUNE 3

"The Advocate, the Holy Spirit, whom the Father will send in my name, will teach you all things and will remind you of everything I have said to you. Peace I leave with you; my peace I give you. I do not give to you as the world gives. Do not let your hearts be troubled and do not be afraid."

John 14:26–27 niv

Jesus, thank You for the Holy Spirit, who helps me, advocates for me, and reminds me of truth from You. Your Spirit within me is the source of real peace.

PRAYER REQUESTS

PRAISES

ANSWERS TO PRAYER

WEDNESDAY, JUNE 4

Rejoice in the Lord always. . . . Let your gentleness be evident to all. The Lord is near. Do not be anxious about anything, but in every situation, by prayer and petition, with thanksgiving, present your requests to God. And the peace of God, which transcends all understanding, will guard your hearts and your minds in Christ Jesus.

PHILIPPIANS 4:4–7 NIV

Praising and thanking You brings me peace, Lord. Remembering You are near brings me peace. Talking with You about all my concerns and needs brings me peace. Lord, help me not to forget these simple and powerful truths.

ANSWERS TO PRAYER

PRAYER REQUESTS

PRAISES

THURSDAY, JUNE 5

"Blessed are the peacemakers, for they shall be called the children of God."
MATTHEW 5:9 SKJV

Remind me that peace doesn't always just happen or suddenly arrive. It has to be *made* with Your help sometimes. And that might involve conflict first. Please guide me and give me wisdom regarding what is good, worthwhile conflict and what is just unnecessary drama. I want Your real, true peace, Lord, not the fake kind so easily found and then lost in this world.

PRAYER REQUESTS

PRAISES

ANSWERS TO PRAYER

FRIDAY, JUNE 6

If it is possible, as far as it depends on you, live at peace with everyone. Do not take revenge, my dear friends, but leave room for God's wrath, for it is written: "It is mine to avenge; I will repay," says the Lord. On the contrary: "If your enemy is hungry, feed him; if he is thirsty, give him something to drink. In doing this, you will heap burning coals on his head." Do not be overcome by evil, but overcome evil with good.
ROMANS 12:18–21 NIV

Lord, please remind me of all the good instruction in Your Word about how to live in peace.

ANSWERS TO PRAYER

PRAYER REQUESTS

PRAISES

SATURDAY, JUNE 7

Make allowance for each other's faults, and forgive anyone who offends you. Remember, the Lord forgave you, so you must forgive others. Above all, clothe yourselves with love, which binds us all together in perfect harmony. And let the peace that comes from Christ rule in your hearts. For as members of one body you are called to live in peace. And always be thankful.
Colossians 3:13–15 nlt

Forgive me, Father, for the times I stir up strife and drama. Help me to obey Your Word and live peacefully and graciously.

PRAYER REQUESTS

PRAISES

ANSWERS TO PRAYER

SUNDAY, JUNE 8

Let the light of Your face shine on us, O Lord. You have filled my heart with more happiness than they have when there is much grain and wine. I will lie down and sleep in peace. O Lord, You alone keep me safe.
PSALM 4:6–8 NLV

Restful, quality sleep is such a gift, Lord. Thank You for blessing me with it because I trust in You. Please keep shining on me, Lord. True happiness, joy, and peace come from no other source than You.

ANSWERS TO PRAYER

PRAYER REQUESTS

PRAISES

MONDAY, JUNE 9

Humble yourselves, therefore, under God's mighty hand, that he may lift you up in due time. Cast all your anxiety on him because he cares for you.

1 PETER 5:6–7 NIV

I bow before You, mighty God. Please remove my pride in thinking I should do things on my own. Anxiety comes from thinking I must have everything under control by myself. You want me to depend on Your care and give You my anxiety. Thank You for exchanging it for Your perfect peace.

PRAYER REQUESTS

PRAISES

ANSWERS TO PRAYER

TUESDAY, JUNE 10

Those who are dominated by the sinful nature think about sinful things, but those who are controlled by the Holy Spirit think about things that please the Spirit. So letting your sinful nature control your mind leads to death. But letting the Spirit control your mind leads to life and peace.

Romans 8:5–6 nlt

Lord, please help me keep my attention away from sinful things that will destroy me. I want Your Holy Spirit in control of my mind, focusing me on all that is good and right and pleasing to You. That's how I can have real peace and joy.

ANSWERS TO PRAYER

PRAYER REQUESTS

PRAISES

WEDNESDAY, JUNE 11

By fearing the Lord, people avoid evil. When people's lives please the Lord, even their enemies are at peace with them.
Proverbs 16:6–7 nlt

Lord, Your Word makes it crystal clear: when I fear You in the right kind of way—with love and respect for You and with obedience to Your commands—I'll avoid evil, bring You glory, and live in peace. There's no better way of life than to live for You!

PRAYER REQUESTS

PRAISES

ANSWERS TO PRAYER

THURSDAY, JUNE 12

"Though the mountains be shaken and the hills be removed, yet my unfailing love for you will not be shaken nor my covenant of peace be removed," says the Lord, who has compassion on you.

Isaiah 54:10 niv

I'm overwhelmed with gratitude knowing that nothing at all in this crazy world can take away Your love and salvation from me, Lord. Thank You for Your mercy and compassion and for filling me with deep, abiding peace.

ANSWERS TO PRAYER

PRAYER REQUESTS

PRAISES

FRIDAY, JUNE 13

When you follow the desires of your sinful nature, the results are very clear: sexual immorality, impurity, lustful pleasures, idolatry, sorcery, hostility, quarreling, jealousy, outbursts of anger, selfish ambition, dissension, division, envy, drunkenness, wild parties, and other sins like these. . . . But the Holy Spirit produces this kind of fruit in our lives: love, joy, peace, patience, kindness, goodness, faithfulness, gentleness, and self-control.
GALATIANS 5:19–23 NLT

Lord, help me to reject any desire of my sinful nature, which will always destroy my peace. I want more and more of the fruit of the Holy Spirit growing in my life.

PRAYER REQUESTS

PRAISES

ANSWERS TO PRAYER

SATURDAY, JUNE 14
Flag Day

Brothers and sisters, rejoice! Strive for full restoration, encourage one another, be of one mind, live in peace. And the God of love and peace will be with you.
2 Corinthians 13:11 niv

Lord, please help all of us who believe in You to rejoice more. In our churches and communities, help us to delight in each other and in our blessings. Help us to get along well and work out conflict quickly. Let us live with great peace and joy and love for one another.

ANSWERS TO PRAYER

PRAYER REQUESTS

PRAISES

SUNDAY, JUNE 15
Father's Day

Those who love your instructions have great peace and do not stumble. I long for your rescue, Lord, so I have obeyed your commands. I have obeyed your laws, for I love them very much. Yes, I obey your commandments and laws because you know everything I do.
Psalm 119:165–168 NLT

Sometimes I wonder why I don't feel peaceful, and then realize how little time I've spent in Your Word lately, Father. Please forgive me and help me be disciplined. I want a renewed love and deep desire to know Your good instructions and commands.

PRAYER REQUESTS

PRAISES

ANSWERS TO PRAYER

MONDAY, JUNE 16

May the God of hope fill you with all joy and peace as you trust in him, so that you may overflow with hope by the power of the Holy Spirit.

ROMANS 15:13 NIV

You know what I'm going through and how it discourages me and gives me anxiety, Lord. Please help. Instead of discouragement, I want to overflow with hope about the issues that are weighing on my mind. Fill me up with joy and peace.

ANSWERS TO PRAYER

PRAYER REQUESTS

PRAISES

TUESDAY, JUNE 17

"Come to Me, all of you who work and have heavy loads. I will give you rest. Follow My teachings and learn from Me. I am gentle and do not have pride. You will have rest for your souls. For My way of carrying a load is easy and My load is not heavy."
MATTHEW 11:28–30 NLV

Jesus, thank You for Your invitation and for Your promise of rest and peace. I feel so very loved knowing that You want to teach me and take away my heavy burdens.

PRAYER REQUESTS

PRAISES

ANSWERS TO PRAYER

WEDNESDAY, JUNE 18

Fix your thoughts on what is true, and honorable, and right, and pure, and lovely, and admirable. Think about things that are excellent and worthy of praise. Keep putting into practice all you learned and received from me—everything you heard from me and saw me doing. Then the God of peace will be with you.

Philippians 4:8–9 nlt

Lord, remind me to keep my mind healthy. If I choose to focus on what's true and right and lovely and pure according to Your Word, I will have increasingly more of those good things in my life. Thank You for showing me how to have true happiness and peace.

ANSWERS TO PRAYER

PRAYER REQUESTS

PRAISES

THURSDAY, JUNE 19

Since we have been made right in God's sight by faith, we have peace with God because of what Jesus Christ our Lord has done for us.
Romans 5:1 NLT

Some people have anxiety wondering if they are ever doing enough to earn their way into heaven. I'm so grateful to have true peace with You, God, because I know I could never do enough. Jesus did it all for me through His death on the cross and His resurrection. He takes my sins away, and because of that, I can be in close relationship with You! What a gift!

PRAYER REQUESTS

PRAISES

ANSWERS TO PRAYER

FRIDAY, JUNE 20
First Day of Summer

"Be still, and know that I am God. I will be exalted among the nations, I will be exalted in the earth!" The Lord of hosts is with us; the God of Jacob is our fortress.
Psalm 46:10–11 esv

I forget far too often to just stop and be still before You, Lord. Forgive me. Remind me that, at any time and in any place, I can quiet my mind and soul and just sit with You, filling up with peace as I focus on all of Your goodness and glory.

ANSWERS TO PRAYER

PRAYER REQUESTS

PRAISES

SATURDAY, JUNE 21

"The Lord disciplines the one he loves, and he chastens everyone he accepts as his son." Endure hardship as discipline; God is treating you as his children. . . . No discipline seems pleasant at the time, but painful. Later on, however, it produces a harvest of righteousness and peace for those who have been trained by it.

Hebrews 12:6–7, 11 niv

Lord, show me where You are disciplining me, and help me to endure and appreciate it. Please encourage me that You are working things out for my good and peace.

PRAYER REQUESTS

PRAISES

ANSWERS TO PRAYER

SUNDAY, JUNE 22

How beautiful on the mountains are the feet of those who bring good news, who proclaim peace, who bring good tidings, who proclaim salvation.
Isaiah 52:7 niv

Lord, remind me how beautiful, how needed it is in this world to bring Your good news of salvation and peace to people who don't yet know You as Savior. Help me to be confident and bold and to share Your truth and love with everyone who will listen.

ANSWERS TO PRAYER

PRAYER REQUESTS

PRAISES

MONDAY, JUNE 23

*Those who are peacemakers will plant seeds of
peace and reap a harvest of righteousness.*
JAMES 3:18 NLT

Lord, help me to be a brave peacemaker—not someone who creates conflict just for the sake of drama but not someone who totally avoids conflict either. I want to make peace in ways that honor You, to help bring truth and justice into hard situations. I sure can't do this well without Your help. I'm trusting and leaning on You.

PRAYER REQUESTS

ANSWERS TO PRAYER

PRAISES

TUESDAY, JUNE 24

Let two or three people prophesy, and let the others evaluate what is said. . . . Remember that people who prophesy are in control of their spirit and can take turns. For God is not a God of disorder but of peace, as in all the meetings of God's holy people.

1 Corinthians 14:29, 32–33 nlt

God of peace, thank You for being a God of order and not chaos. Help me bring Your holy order into every situation and relationship.

ANSWERS TO PRAYER

PRAYER REQUESTS

PRAISES

WEDNESDAY, JUNE 25

He took up our pain and bore our suffering. . . . He was pierced for our transgressions, he was crushed for our iniquities; the punishment that brought us peace was on him, and by his wounds we are healed.

Isaiah 53:4–5 niv

Jesus, I don't want to forget that the reason I can have true peace is because You took the punishment for my sin. You paid the price of death on the cross for me. I don't deserve Your love and grace, yet You give it so generously. With deep gratitude, I trust in You alone as Savior and will do my best to live for You!

PRAYER REQUESTS

PRAISES

ANSWERS TO PRAYER

THURSDAY, JUNE 26

Blessed are those who find wisdom, those who gain understanding, for she is more profitable than silver and yields better returns than gold. She is more precious than rubies; nothing you desire can compare with her. Long life is in her right hand; in her left hand are riches and honor. Her ways are pleasant ways, and all her paths are peace.
PROVERBS 3:13–17 NIV

Lord, I want to follow the peaceful paths in life—the ones You set me on when I seek Your wisdom.

ANSWERS TO PRAYER

PRAYER REQUESTS

PRAISES

FRIDAY, JUNE 27

I urge you, first of all, to pray for all people. Ask God to help them; intercede on their behalf, and give thanks for them. Pray this way for kings and all who are in authority so that we can live peaceful and quiet lives marked by godliness and dignity. This is good and pleases God our Savior, who wants everyone to be saved and to understand the truth.
1 Timothy 2:1–4 nlt

Lord, forgive me for not spending more time in prayer for the leaders over our nation. Let their hearts and minds be receptive to Your truth and wisdom. Help them to lead us in peaceful ways that honor You.

PRAYER REQUESTS

PRAISES

ANSWERS TO PRAYER

SATURDAY, JUNE 28

"If you want to enjoy life and see many happy days, keep your tongue from speaking evil and your lips from telling lies. Turn away from evil and do good. Search for peace, and work to maintain it. The eyes of the Lord watch over those who do right, and his ears are open to their prayers. But the Lord turns his face against those who do evil."

1 Peter 3:10–12 NLT

Your Word tells me how to enjoy life and be happy. Please help me to constantly turn away from evil and cultivate true peace, honesty, and goodness that come from You, Lord.

ANSWERS TO PRAYER

PRAYER REQUESTS

PRAISES

SUNDAY, JUNE 29

Walk in a manner worthy of the calling to which you have been called, with all humility and gentleness, with patience, bearing with one another in love, eager to maintain the unity of the Spirit in the bond of peace. There is one body and one Spirit—just as you were called to the one hope that belongs to your call—one Lord, one faith, one baptism, one God and Father of all, who is over all and through all and in all.

Ephesians 4:1–6 esv

Father, remind me of the importance of unity and peace among Your people. Help me to be eager to maintain and inspire unity and peace.

PRAYER REQUESTS

PRAISES

ANSWERS TO PRAYER

MONDAY, JUNE 30

The Lord sits enthroned as king forever. May the Lord give strength to his people! May the Lord bless his people with peace!
Psalm 29:10–11 esv

Because You are sovereign, Lord, all who trust in You can have supernatural strength and peace. You sit on the throne above all of our universe. You are King and Savior. You see all and know all, and You love and provide for and protect Your people. I'm so grateful.

ANSWERS TO PRAYER

PRAYER REQUESTS

PRAISES

JULY
Freedom in Christ

For the Lord is the Spirit, and wherever the Spirit of the Lord is, there is freedom.
2 CORINTHIANS 3:17 NLT

SUNDAY	MONDAY	TUESDAY	WEDNESDAY	THURSDAY	FRIDAY	SATURDAY
		1	2	3	4 Independence Day	5
6	7	8	9	10	11	12
13	14	15	16	17	18	19
20	21	22	23	24	25	26
27	28	29	30	31		

When Jesus came to earth, God's children lived under the restrictions of the Law. In theory, salvation *was* possible, but the crushing weight of the rules and regulations meant that no one could stand blameless before God. But Christ's death on the cross provided a new way—freedom through His grace—once and for all time!

TUESDAY, JULY 1

Brothers and sisters, God has called you to freedom! Hear the call, and do not spoil this gift by using your liberty to engage in what your flesh desires; instead, use it to serve each other as Jesus taught through love.

GALATIANS 5:13 VOICE

Give me the correct perspective of freedom, God. You've graciously made me free through Your Son, and I don't want to use that freedom incorrectly. Give me a heart for other people and I will do whatever I can to love them in Your name.

ANSWERS TO PRAYER

PRAYER REQUESTS

PRAISES

WEDNESDAY, JULY 2

So stand strong for our freedom! The Anointed One freed us so we wouldn't spend one more day under the yoke of slavery, trapped under the law.

GALATIANS 5:1 VOICE

I refuse to be enslaved by anyone or anything, Jesus, because now that I've experienced Your freedom, I don't want to live any other way. So I will be bold in encouraging others to reject the lie that we must check off to-do lists to earn Your favor. I want everyone to know what true freedom in Christ means!

PRAYER REQUESTS

PRAISES

ANSWERS TO PRAYER

THURSDAY, JULY 3

Give your burdens to the Lord, and he will take care of you. He will not permit the godly to slip and fall.
Psalm 55:22 nlt

When I'm struggling to stay upright on the path You've laid before me, Father, help me to realize that I'm carrying too much. You are faithful to lift the weight that's dragging me down, and I give it to You now.

ANSWERS TO PRAYER

PRAYER REQUESTS

PRAISES

FRIDAY, JULY 4
Independence Day

"So if the Son sets you free, you will be free indeed."
JOHN 8:36 ESV

Jesus, the freedom You've given me is lasting. Forever, without an expiration date. Signed, sealed, delivered with a (more than) lifetime guarantee. It's a full freedom that covers every aspect of my life—both the physical and spiritual. Help me live in that freedom every moment and live in such a way that others are attracted to You. I will not squander such a precious gift!

PRAYER REQUESTS

PRAISES

ANSWERS TO PRAYER

SATURDAY, JULY 5

You say, "I am allowed to do anything"—but not everything is good for you. And even though "I am allowed to do anything," I must not become a slave to anything.

1 Corinthians 6:12 NLT

Give me Your view of true freedom, Jesus. May I never be guilty of using the freedom You've given me to do things that dishonor You. Just because I'm *allowed* to do something doesn't mean that I *should*. Give me Your wisdom and perspective so everything I do glorifies You.

ANSWERS TO PRAYER

PRAYER REQUESTS

PRAISES

SUNDAY, JULY 6

So you must realize, my brothers, that through this resurrected man forgiveness of sins is assured to you. Through Jesus, everyone who believes is set free from all sins—sins which the law of Moses could not release you from.
ACTS 13:38–39 VOICE

I know what it feels like to live in guilt and shame, Lord. And I know the relief that Your forgiveness provides. Thank You for providing freedom that truly means everything to me. Help me to live in such a way that others see it and want to experience it too.

PRAYER REQUESTS

PRAISES

ANSWERS TO PRAYER

MONDAY, JULY 7

Out of my distress I called on the Lord; the Lord answered me and set me free.
Psalm 118:5 esv

Father, You heard me cry out when I was shackled to my sin. I did everything I knew to free myself, but I was powerless against sin's hold on my life. I tried to "be good" and that only lasted so long. But Your freedom through salvation is truly the key that unlocked the chains forever. I will praise You for as long as I live!

ANSWERS TO PRAYER

PRAYER REQUESTS

PRAISES

TUESDAY, JULY 8

The power of the Holy Spirit has made me free from the power of sin and death. This power is mine because I belong to Christ Jesus.
ROMANS 8:2 NLV

Jesus, when I feel tempted to fall back into my old, sinful ways, remind me that it was the power of the Holy Spirit that conquered sin and death. It was the Holy Spirit who resurrected Your body from the grave. No person and no power can make me a slave anymore!

PRAYER REQUESTS

PRAISES

ANSWERS TO PRAYER

WEDNESDAY, JULY 9

Don't you realize that you become the slave of whatever you choose to obey? You can be a slave to sin, which leads to death, or you can choose to obey God, which leads to righteous living.

Romans 6:16 NLT

You've given me free will to do what I choose, Lord. And I choose to obey You. My obedience is not out of obligation or guilt. I obey You because I love You. You have been so good to me, and I know my obedience pleases You and You will bless me for it.

ANSWERS TO PRAYER

PRAYER REQUESTS

PRAISES

THURSDAY, JULY 10

For God has not given us a spirit of fear and timidity, but of power, love, and self-discipline.

2 Timothy 1:7 NLT

I will not be a slave to fear, Father. I know what that feels like, and I know how crippling it is. Instead, I choose to live in Your freedom. You have given me the power of the Holy Spirit, who leads me in love. You've given me the ability to wisely discern Your will, and I will walk on the path You have laid before me.

PRAYER REQUESTS

PRAISES

ANSWERS TO PRAYER

FRIDAY, JULY 11

Sin is no longer your master, for you no longer live under the requirements of the law. Instead, you live under the freedom of God's grace.
ROMANS 6:14 NLT

Father, I am so grateful that You are a God of order. But I'm even more grateful that You are a God of grace, not legalism. You command me to love You and love others, and while I'm imperfect at both, I know You are faithful to help me do Your will.

ANSWERS TO PRAYER

PRAYER REQUESTS

PRAISES

SATURDAY, JULY 12

Since you are free to do as you please, be careful that this does not hurt a weak Christian.
1 Corinthians 8:9 nlv

Give me a heart that is sensitive and cares about the people around me, Lord. I know that Your grace gives me great freedom to choose how I live out my life in Your will, but I don't want to live in a way that may give new Christians a wrong impression of You. Help me make wise decisions, Lord.

PRAYER REQUESTS

PRAISES

ANSWERS TO PRAYER

SUNDAY, JULY 13

"The Spirit of the Lord. . .has sent me to proclaim that captives will be released, that the blind will see, that the oppressed will be set free, and that the time of the Lord's favor has come."
Luke 4:18–19 nlt

Jesus, help me fully understand that I am not a slave in my present circumstances. No matter what difficult times come, the truth is that You have already overcome them. Help me to live a life that demonstrates that You are redeeming and perfecting everything—even the hard things!

ANSWERS TO PRAYER

PRAYER REQUESTS

PRAISES

MONDAY, JULY 14

The Spirit you received does not make you slaves, so that you live in fear again; rather, the Spirit you received brought about your adoption to sonship. And by him we cry, "Abba, Father."
Romans 8:15 niv

I belong to You, Lord. But not in a slavery way—in a loving and supportive family way! You are my spiritual Father, who *chose me* to be a part of Your family. That fact makes me feel very loved and very safe.

PRAYER REQUESTS

PRAISES

ANSWERS TO PRAYER

TUESDAY, JULY 15

For when we died with Christ we were set free from the power of sin. And since we died with Christ, we know we will also live with him.
Romans 6:7–8 NLT

Jesus, I don't fear death, because I know You've conquered it. And I'm not afraid of my old, sinful self dying with You, because I already know the end of the story of Your physical death—You came to life again! Thank You for taking care of the entirety of death, once and for all!

ANSWERS TO PRAYER

PRAYER REQUESTS

PRAISES

WEDNESDAY, JULY 16

We are allowed to do anything, but not everything is good for us to do. We are allowed to do anything, but not all things help us grow strong as Christians.
1 Corinthians 10:23 NLV

Lord, give me clear understanding of the details and decisions of life that will help me grow stronger in my faith. I don't want to just spin my wheels while I live on earth. I want to grow mature and strong and closer to You. Clear the path You want me to take.

PRAYER REQUESTS

PRAISES

ANSWERS TO PRAYER

THURSDAY, JULY 17

"God sent his Son into the world not to judge the world, but to save the world through him."

JOHN 3:17 NLT

Jesus, You had every right to come into the world and pass judgment on every person You came across. But You didn't. You chose to see them as beloved brothers and sisters who are priceless to Your heavenly Father. Thank You for seeing the same in me, and thank You for Your sacrifice on the cross.

ANSWERS TO PRAYER

PRAYER REQUESTS

PRAISES

FRIDAY, JULY 18

So I say, let the Holy Spirit guide your lives. Then you won't be doing what your sinful nature craves.

GALATIANS 5:16 NLT

Holy Spirit, please guide me in the big decisions and small choices that dictate my day-to-day life. Give me a sincere desire to follow the will and way of God so that my life will be a testament to His glory. I will live in eager anticipation of Your prompting because I know when I feel You move, I'm being nudged in the right direction.

PRAYER REQUESTS

PRAISES

ANSWERS TO PRAYER

SATURDAY, JULY 19

"I have been crucified with Christ and I no longer live, but Christ lives in me. The life I now live in the body, I live by faith in the Son of God, who loved me and gave himself for me."

GALATIANS 2:20 NIV

Jesus, before You came into my life, I had no foundation and no direction. By faith, I now follow Your Spirit inside me, living the best I can in Your freedom every day until You return.

ANSWERS TO PRAYER

PRAYER REQUESTS

PRAISES

SUNDAY, JULY 20

The rich rules over the poor, and the borrower is the slave of the lender.
PROVERBS 22:7 ESV

Lord, the financial debts I have are not a blessing to me. Sometimes I feel bound and gagged by the monthly payment and the interest. Please give me the wisdom I need to make a plan to quickly pay back what I owe so that I can experience financial freedom where I can be more generous with all that You have given me.

PRAYER REQUESTS

ANSWERS TO PRAYER

PRAISES

MONDAY, JULY 21

"Come to me, all you who are weary and burdened, and I will give you rest. Take my yoke upon you and learn from me, for I am gentle and humble in heart, and you will find rest for your souls."

MATTHEW 11:28–29 NIV

I'm ready to hand over the burdens of life, Lord. I long for the rest You promise, so please take the worries and anxious thoughts that I can't seem to work through myself. Thank You, Lord.

ANSWERS TO PRAYER

PRAYER REQUESTS

PRAISES

TUESDAY, JULY 22

I will walk in freedom, for I have devoted myself to your commandments.
Psalm 119:45 nlt

Father, I no longer view Your commands as an oppressive list of rules and regulations. That's what they were under the old covenant, but under the freedom of Jesus, I seek to honor You by following what You want me to do. I will not be perfect, but I know I'm perfectly loved and covered by Your grace.

PRAYER REQUESTS

PRAISES

ANSWERS TO PRAYER

WEDNESDAY, JULY 23

*Don't worry about anything; instead, pray about everything.
Tell God what you need, and thank him for all he has done.*

Philippians 4:6 nlt

Some days I feel like a slave to my worries, Lord. But I know that's a slavery of my own making. Instead of worrying, I will do what You tell me to do: pray about it. And in the same breath, I will thank You for everything You've blessed me with—because it's a lot!

ANSWERS TO PRAYER

PRAYER REQUESTS

PRAISES

THURSDAY, JULY 24

So bow down under God's strong hand; then when the time comes, God will lift you up. Since God cares for you, let Him carry all your burdens and worries.
1 Peter 5:6–7 voice

I trust You with my life, God. I trust You with my loved ones. I trust You with the stress that keeps me up at night. Please take my anxiety. I can't deal with it on my own, but I know You will handle it and equip me to live boldly in Your name.

PRAYER REQUESTS

PRAISES

ANSWERS TO PRAYER

FRIDAY, JULY 25

Do not seek revenge; instead, allow God's wrath to make sure justice is served. Turn it over to Him. For the Scriptures say, "Revenge is Mine. I will settle all scores."
Romans 12:19 voice

When I see so much injustice in the world, God, I can quickly get discouraged and burdened. But Your Word tells me that it's not my responsibility to see that justice is served. . .it's Yours. So when I see wrongs happening, remind me that You will settle all scores.

ANSWERS TO PRAYER

PRAYER REQUESTS

PRAISES

SATURDAY, JULY 26

Praise the Lord; praise God our savior! For each day he carries us in his arms.
Psalm 68:19 nlt

I remember what it felt like to be carried by a parent on a hike through the woods, Lord. It was so comforting! My tired little legs didn't have to keep up with my parents' long strides. I didn't have to look out for rocks and roots I might trip on. I could freely enjoy nature and conversation with the parent whose arms firmly held me—just as You do now.

PRAYER REQUESTS

PRAISES

ANSWERS TO PRAYER

SUNDAY, JULY 27

Put on the full armor of God, so that when the day of evil comes, you may be able to stand your ground, and after you have done everything, to stand.
EPHESIANS 6:13 NIV

God, please help me to do the prep work necessary to combat evil that attacks me. Whether it's through circumstances, health issues, relationships, spiritual warfare, or my own anxious thoughts, give me the foundation to stand firmly in Your love and Your Word. I know You will give me the strength I need.

ANSWERS TO PRAYER

PRAYER REQUESTS

PRAISES

MONDAY, JULY 28

Jesus Christ is the same yesterday and today and forever.
HEBREWS 13:8 NLV

Life brings so many changes, Jesus. Careers shift, relationships morph, family dynamics change, youth and health deteriorate. Yet through every season, every bump in the road, every twist and turn, You remain the same. Thank You for this truth. Thank You for the comfort I have in knowing I don't have to wonder if Your love for me has changed. When everything else changes, You remain constant!

PRAYER REQUESTS

PRAISES

ANSWERS TO PRAYER

TUESDAY, JULY 29

"The Helper is the Holy Spirit. The Father will send Him in My place. He will teach you everything and help you remember everything I have told you."

John 14:26 nlv

Jesus, thank You for the gift of the Holy Spirit. I know that when I am listening to the Spirit, I feel rooted and strong in my faith and in Your love. There's freedom in knowing I am secure today and for all eternity—and it's the Holy Spirit who gives me that assurance.

ANSWERS TO PRAYER

PRAYER REQUESTS

PRAISES

WEDNESDAY, JULY 30

Don't let anyone capture you with empty philosophies and high-sounding nonsense that come from human thinking and from the spiritual powers of this world, rather than from Christ.

COLOSSIANS 2:8 NLT

God, please guard my heart and my mind from the "wisdom" that this world and the devil are trying to sell as truth. I need the Holy Spirit to send up a red flag when something doesn't align with God's wisdom. Give me discernment to understand Your Word in every aspect of my life.

PRAYER REQUESTS

PRAISES

ANSWERS TO PRAYER

THURSDAY, JULY 31

If we confess our sins, he is faithful and just and will forgive us our sins and purify us from all unrighteousness.
1 John 1:9 niv

A clean slate gives me such a sense of freedom, Lord. When I confess and repent, guilt can no longer hold me captive to my sins. Thank You for being the God of forgiveness, Lord. I am never afraid to admit a wrong to You, because I know it strengthens the bond of grace between us.

ANSWERS TO PRAYER

PRAYER REQUESTS

PRAISES

AUGUST
Seeking God's Wisdom

If any of you lacks wisdom, let him ask God, who gives generously to all without reproach, and it will be given him.
JAMES 1:5 ESV

SUNDAY	MONDAY	TUESDAY	WEDNESDAY	THURSDAY	FRIDAY	SATURDAY
					1	2
3	4	5	6	7	8	9
10	11	12	13	14	15	16
17	18	19	20	21	22	23
24	25	26	27	28	29	30
31						

God is not up in the heavens hoarding all the wisdom. He's eager to share. He certainly knows we need it in this sin-filled world. And so we must ask Him and trust Him and then apply His wisdom to all of our daily doings.

FRIDAY, AUGUST 1

If you need wisdom, ask our generous God, and he will give it to you. . . . But when you ask him, be sure that your faith is in God alone. Do not waver, for a person with divided loyalty is as unsettled as a wave of the sea that is blown and tossed by the wind. Such people should not expect to receive anything from the Lord. Their loyalty is divided between God and the world, and they are unstable in everything they do.
JAMES 1:5–8 NLT

Your wisdom is the only wisdom I need, Lord. My faith is in You alone.

ANSWERS TO PRAYER

PRAYER REQUESTS

PRAISES

SATURDAY, AUGUST 2

The word of God is alive and powerful. It is sharper than the sharpest two-edged sword, cutting between soul and spirit, between joint and marrow. It exposes our innermost thoughts and desires. Nothing in all creation is hidden from God. Everything is naked and exposed before his eyes, and he is the one to whom we are accountable.

Hebrews 4:12–13 NLT

Heavenly Father, please speak directly to me through Your living and powerful Word every day. Guide me in wisdom and truth, and help me to listen and obey well.

PRAYER REQUESTS

PRAISES

ANSWERS TO PRAYER

SUNDAY, AUGUST 3

"People are like the grass. Their beauty fades as quickly as the flowers in a field. The grass withers and the flowers fade beneath the breath of the Lord. And so it is with people. The grass withers and the flowers fade, but the word of our God stands forever."

Isaiah 40:6–8 nlt

It makes no sense to follow wisdom from the world, which changes and fades just like people do. I want to follow the unchanging eternal wisdom that comes from You and Your Word, Father God.

ANSWERS TO PRAYER

PRAYER REQUESTS

PRAISES

MONDAY, AUGUST 4

If anyone is a hearer of the word and not a doer, he is like a man who looks intently at his natural face in a mirror. For he looks at himself and goes away and at once forgets what he was like. But the one who looks into the perfect law, the law of liberty, and perseveres, being no hearer who forgets but a doer who acts, he will be blessed in his doing.

James 1:23–25 esv

Lord, remind me regularly that wisdom doesn't come from just hearing Your Word and storing it up and doing nothing with it. Help me to be a *doer* of Your truth and love and wisdom.

PRAYER REQUESTS

PRAISES

ANSWERS TO PRAYER

TUESDAY, AUGUST 5

But the wisdom from above is first of all pure. It is also peace loving, gentle at all times, and willing to yield to others. It is full of mercy and the fruit of good deeds. It shows no favoritism and is always sincere.

JAMES 3:17 NLT

You give instruction on what real wisdom from You is, Lord. Help me to filter everything that the world says is wisdom through what Your Word says is wisdom. Your Word is always truth.

ANSWERS TO PRAYER

PRAYER REQUESTS

PRAISES

WEDNESDAY, AUGUST 6

Pray about everything.
Philippians 4:6 nlv

These are three words in scripture I should never ever forget! Thank You so much that there is nothing that is too small, too insignificant, for me to pray about, Lord. Your Word literally tells me to ask You for Your help and guidance with everything going on in my life and home and family and relationships and in the world around me. You want me to seek Your wisdom in it all, and I'm so very grateful.

PRAYER REQUESTS

ANSWERS TO PRAYER

PRAISES

THURSDAY, AUGUST 7

Come close to God and He will come close to you. Wash your hands, you sinners. Clean up your hearts, you who want to follow the sinful ways of the world and God at the same time. Be sorry for your sins. . . . Let yourself be brought low before the Lord. Then He will lift you up and help you.

James 4:8–10 nlv

Asking for wisdom without being humble is foolish. Please rid me of my pride, Lord. I constantly need Your forgiveness of my sins, and I depend on You for everything. Every good thing in my life is a gift from You.

ANSWERS TO PRAYER

PRAYER REQUESTS

PRAISES

FRIDAY, AUGUST 8

And the disciples came and said to Him, "Why do You speak to them in parables?" He answered and said to them, "Because it is given to you to know the mysteries of the kingdom of heaven, but to them it is not given. For whoever has, to him more shall be given, and he shall have abundance. But whoever does not have, even what he has shall be taken away from him. Therefore I speak to them in parables, because seeing they do not see, and hearing they do not hear, nor do they understand."
MATTHEW 13:10–13 SKJV

Jesus, help me to study and understand Your parables.

PRAYER REQUESTS

PRAISES

ANSWERS TO PRAYER

SATURDAY, AUGUST 9

I will be careful to live a blameless life—when will you come to help me? I will lead a life of integrity in my own home. I will refuse to look at anything vile and vulgar.
Psalm 101:2–3 nlt

Lord, what a challenging goal it is to avoid anything vile and vulgar in this world. Please help me. I want to be wise and avoid sin. I want to live with integrity to honor You and point people to salvation in You.

ANSWERS TO PRAYER

PRAYER REQUESTS

PRAISES

SUNDAY, AUGUST 10

These are the proverbs of Solomon, David's son, king of Israel. Their purpose is to teach people wisdom and discipline, to help them understand the insights of the wise. Their purpose is to teach people to live disciplined and successful lives, to help them do what is right, just, and fair. . . . Let the wise listen to these proverbs and become even wiser.

Proverbs 1:1–3, 5 NLT

Lord, keep urging me to come back to the book of Proverbs regularly in my life. I want to be consistent in Your wisdom and discipline.

PRAYER REQUESTS

PRAISES

ANSWERS TO PRAYER

MONDAY, AUGUST 11

Let us hold unswervingly to the hope we profess, for he who promised is faithful. And let us consider how we may spur one another on toward love and good deeds, not giving up meeting together, as some are in the habit of doing, but encouraging one another—and all the more as you see the Day approaching.
HEBREWS 10:23–25 NIV

Lord, thank You for the encouragement and wisdom I gain from fellowship with other believers who love You and learn from You too.

ANSWERS TO PRAYER

PRAYER REQUESTS

PRAISES

TUESDAY, AUGUST 12

Let the message about Christ, in all its richness, fill your lives. Teach and counsel each other with all the wisdom he gives. Sing psalms and hymns and spiritual songs to God with thankful hearts. And whatever you do or say, do it as a representative of the Lord Jesus, giving thanks through him to God the Father.
Colossians 3:16–17 NLT

Jesus, I want to be a good representative of You, helping others want to know and love You as their Savior too.

PRAYER REQUESTS

PRAISES

ANSWERS TO PRAYER

WEDNESDAY, AUGUST 13

You have been taught the holy Scriptures from childhood, and they have given you the wisdom to receive the salvation that comes by trusting in Christ Jesus. All Scripture is inspired by God and is useful to teach us what is true and to make us realize what is wrong in our lives. It corrects us when we are wrong and teaches us to do what is right. God uses it to prepare and equip his people to do every good work.
2 Timothy 3:15–17 NLT

Thank You for Your trustworthy and powerful Word, God!

ANSWERS TO PRAYER

PRAYER REQUESTS

PRAISES

THURSDAY, AUGUST 14

Be angry and do not sin; do not let the sun go down on your anger, and give no opportunity to the devil.

Ephesians 4:26–27 ESV

Father, I need extra doses of wisdom when I feel angry. Help me not to sin when I'm upset, which is so hard! But I want to cool down first and then take action if needed with Your good guidance leading the way.

PRAYER REQUESTS

PRAISES

ANSWERS TO PRAYER

FRIDAY, AUGUST 15

You make known to me the path of life; in your presence there is fullness of joy; at your right hand are pleasures forevermore.

Psalm 16:11 ESV

Lord, I seek Your wisdom to know the difference between temporary happiness and eternal joy. The world offers me all kinds of ways to be happy for a little while, but only You offer the path of life that leads to life and joy forever in Your presence.

ANSWERS TO PRAYER

PRAYER REQUESTS

PRAISES

SATURDAY, AUGUST 16

O Lord, You have looked through me and have known me. You know when I sit down and when I get up. You understand my thoughts from far away. You look over my path and my lying down. You know all my ways very well. Even before I speak a word, O Lord, You know it all.

Psalm 139:1–4 nlv

Lord, You see and know everything about me, far better than I even know myself. Show me my strengths and weaknesses. Reveal my sins to me and help me repent. Let me use the gifts and talents You have given me to serve and glorify You.

PRAYER REQUESTS

PRAISES

ANSWERS TO PRAYER

SUNDAY, AUGUST 17

Mary sat at the feet of Jesus and listened to all He said. Martha was working hard getting the supper ready. . . . Jesus said to her, "Martha, Martha, you are worried and troubled about many things. Only a few things are important, even just one. Mary has chosen the good thing. It will not be taken away from her."
Luke 10:39–42 nlv

Jesus, I need wisdom for finding the right balance between working to honor You and taking time to be still in Your presence and learn from You.

ANSWERS TO PRAYER

PRAYER REQUESTS

PRAISES

MONDAY, AUGUST 18

We have come to know and to believe the love that God has for us. God is love, and whoever abides in love abides in God, and God abides in him. By this is love perfected with us, so that we may have confidence for the day of judgment, because as he is so also are we in this world.

1 John 4:16–17 ESV

I need wisdom about what real love is, God, and You are love itself. I need more knowledge and relationship with You through Your unchanging Word to truly love others.

PRAYER REQUESTS

ANSWERS TO PRAYER

PRAISES

TUESDAY, AUGUST 19

Do not let your beauty come from the outside. It should not be the way you comb your hair or the wearing of gold or the wearing of fine clothes. Your beauty should come from the inside. It should come from the heart. This is the kind that lasts. Your beauty should be a gentle and quiet spirit. In God's sight this is of great worth and no amount of money can buy it.
1 Peter 3:3–4 nlv

Lord, please encourage me with wisdom about what true beauty in Your eyes means. Your view is what really matters.

ANSWERS TO PRAYER

PRAYER REQUESTS

PRAISES

WEDNESDAY, AUGUST 20

Do not be misled: "Bad company corrupts good character." Come back to your senses as you ought, and stop sinning.
1 Corinthians 15:33–34 niv

Father, please forgive me for choosing bad company at times. I need Your wisdom in my friendships. Help me to share Your truth and love with others who need You yet also be wise and avoid people who seek to draw me away from You.

PRAYER REQUESTS

PRAISES

ANSWERS TO PRAYER

THURSDAY, AUGUST 21

Physical training is of some value, but godliness has value for all things, holding promise for both the present life and the life to come. . . . That is why we labor and strive, because we have put our hope in the living God, who is the Savior of all people, and especially of those who believe.

1 Timothy 4:8, 10 niv

Of course it's important to be healthy and physically fit, but please help me to remember that godliness is even more important. When I focus on loving and honoring You first in my life, Lord, everything else falls wisely into place.

ANSWERS TO PRAYER

PRAYER REQUESTS

PRAISES

FRIDAY, AUGUST 22

Happy is the man who finds wisdom, and the man who gets understanding. For it is better than getting silver and fine gold. She is worth more than stones of great worth. Nothing you can wish for compares with her. Long life is in her right hand. Riches and honor are in her left hand. Her ways are pleasing, and all her paths are peace. She is a tree of life to those who take hold of her. Happy are all who hold her near. The Lord built the earth by wisdom.
PROVERBS 3:13–19 NLV

What a treasure it is to have wisdom. Please bless me with it all my life, Lord.

PRAYER REQUESTS

PRAISES

ANSWERS TO PRAYER

SATURDAY, AUGUST 23

For we are God's handiwork, created in Christ Jesus to do good works, which God prepared in advance for us to do.
Ephesians 2:10 niv

Lord, help me not to strive after goals that aren't what You have planned and equipped me for. You created and designed me with good works in mind, and I want to follow Your lead. Nothing I do will ever feel truly fulfilling unless it matches what You have prepared in advance for me to do.

ANSWERS TO PRAYER

PRAYER REQUESTS

PRAISES

SUNDAY, AUGUST 24

Be careful how you live. Don't live like fools, but like those who are wise. Make the most of every opportunity in these evil days. Don't act thoughtlessly, but understand what the Lord wants you to do. Don't be drunk with wine, because that will ruin your life. Instead, be filled with the Holy Spirit, singing psalms and hymns and spiritual songs among yourselves, and making music to the Lord in your hearts.
Ephesians 5:15–19 nlt

Lord, I want to live wisely in ways that bring glory and honor to You!

PRAYER REQUESTS

PRAISES

ANSWERS TO PRAYER

MONDAY, AUGUST 25

Do not deceive yourselves. If any of you think you are wise by the standards of this age, you should become "fools" so that you may become wise. For the wisdom of this world is foolishness in God's sight.
1 Corinthians 3:18–19 niv

Father, help me to be able to discern between what the world calls wisdom and what You call wisdom. I can only do that by constantly learning from and living by the truth in Your Word.

ANSWERS TO PRAYER

PRAYER REQUESTS

PRAISES

TUESDAY, AUGUST 26

Whatever you do, work at it with all your heart, as working for the Lord, not for human masters, since you know that you will receive an inheritance from the Lord as a reward. It is the Lord Christ you are serving.

Colossians 3:23–24 niv

Help me to view whatever work I'm doing with wisdom and joy, Lord. Ultimately, it's all for You. Everything I do can be an act of worship of You when I choose the right attitude.

PRAYER REQUESTS

PRAISES

ANSWERS TO PRAYER

WEDNESDAY, AUGUST 27

We need such a Religious Leader Who made the way for man to go to God. . . . [Jesus] has never sinned and is different from sinful men. . . . Christ is not like other religious leaders. They had to give gifts every day on the altar in worship for their own sins first and then for the sins of the people. Christ did not have to do that. He gave one gift on the altar and that gift was Himself. It was done once and it was for all time.
Hebrews 7:26–27 nlv

Jesus, help me communicate wisely with others who believe in false religions. You alone are the way, truth, and life (John 14:6).

ANSWERS TO PRAYER

PRAYER REQUESTS

PRAISES

THURSDAY, AUGUST 28

People can tame all kinds of animals, birds, reptiles, and fish, but no one can tame the tongue. It is restless and evil, full of deadly poison. Sometimes it praises our Lord and Father, and sometimes it curses those who have been made in the image of God. And so blessing and cursing come pouring out of the same mouth. Surely, my brothers and sisters, this is not right!
JAMES 3:7–10 NLT

Lord, please forgive my many mistakes with my words. I need Your instruction every day about how important it is to wisely watch what I say.

PRAYER REQUESTS

PRAISES

ANSWERS TO PRAYER

FRIDAY, AUGUST 29

"Teacher, which is the great commandment in the Law?" And he said to him, "You shall love the Lord your God with all your heart and with all your soul and with all your mind. This is the great and first commandment. And a second is like it: You shall love your neighbor as yourself. On these two commandments depend all the Law and the Prophets."
MATTHEW 22:36–40 ESV

Jesus, I want to be wise and obey Your commands. Help me never to forget Your two greatest commandments.

ANSWERS TO PRAYER

PRAYER REQUESTS

PRAISES

SATURDAY, AUGUST 30

My being safe and my honor rest with God. My safe place is in God, the rock of my strength. Trust in Him at all times, O people. Pour out your heart before Him. God is a safe place for us.
Psalm 62:7–8 nlv

I need to take precautions in this broken world to be safe, of course, Lord. But please give me wisdom and remind me that You alone are my ultimate safe place and protection. My life is in Your hands.

PRAYER REQUESTS

ANSWERS TO PRAYER

PRAISES

SUNDAY, AUGUST 31

Just as sin ruled over all people and brought them to death, now God's wonderful grace rules instead, giving us right standing with God and resulting in eternal life through Jesus Christ our Lord. Well then, should we keep on sinning so that God can show us more and more of his wonderful grace? Of course not! Since we have died to sin, how can we continue to live in it?
Romans 5:21–6:2 NLT

Lord, please give me wisdom to never take advantage of Your generous grace.

ANSWERS TO PRAYER

PRAYER REQUESTS

PRAISES

SEPTEMBER

Prayers for God's Harvest

"Ask the Lord of the harvest to send more workers into His harvest field."
MATTHEW 9:38 VOICE

SUNDAY	MONDAY	TUESDAY	WEDNESDAY	THURSDAY	FRIDAY	SATURDAY
	1 Labor Day	2	3	4	5	6
7	8	9	10	11	12	13
14	15	16	17	18	19	20
21	22 First Day of Autumn	23	24	25	26	27
28	29	30				

Jesus used a harvest metaphor to illustrate the kingdom of God. The field workers in Matthew 9:38 are not just "professional" missionaries and ministry workers. Our Father chooses to gather the lost through those of us He has already saved. Who in your circle is growing, seeking, and ready to be harvested into the kingdom?

MONDAY, SEPTEMBER 1
Labor Day

And then he told them, "Go into all the world and preach the Good News to everyone."

MARK 16:15 NLT

Jesus, it's amazing that You ask me to help grow Your kingdom. Instead of thinking of it as a burden or an extra responsibility, I choose to consider it a privilege to share Your message with others. Give me eyes to see opportunities to share Your love with everyone I meet, both in the words I say and through my actions.

ANSWERS TO PRAYER

PRAYER REQUESTS

PRAISES

TUESDAY, SEPTEMBER 2

"You will receive power when the Holy Spirit comes upon you. And you will be my witnesses, telling people about me everywhere—in Jerusalem, throughout Judea, in Samaria, and to the ends of the earth."

Acts 1:8 nlt

Lord, thank You for the gift of Your Holy Spirit. Alone, I am afraid to share Your message with others, but with the help and power of Your Spirit, I feel confident and capable of being Your representative to everyone I meet!

PRAYER REQUESTS

PRAISES

ANSWERS TO PRAYER

WEDNESDAY, SEPTEMBER 3

The Lord has commanded us to do this. Remember His words: I have appointed you a light to the nations beyond Israel, so you can bring redemption to every corner of the earth.
ACTS 13:47 VOICE

When this world feels extra dark, God, please shine all the brighter in me. Because when Your light shines, darkness flees. Give me the courage to stand tall and shine Your light in all directions—as a lighthouse beacon for others to find Your light and love.

ANSWERS TO PRAYER

PRAYER REQUESTS

PRAISES

THURSDAY, SEPTEMBER 4

*"Tell of His greatness among the nations.
Tell of His great works among all the people."*
1 Chronicles 16:24 nlv

When I feel fumbling and ineloquent in sharing my faith with others, Lord, remind me that all I'm doing is talking about what You have done in my life. From the soul-saving work of my salvation to the little daily blessings You send my way, anything I share with someone else proclaims Your greatness and can plant seeds in the hearts around me.

PRAYER REQUESTS

PRAISES

ANSWERS TO PRAYER

FRIDAY, SEPTEMBER 5

*And how can anyone preach unless they are sent? As it is written:
"How beautiful are the feet of those who bring good news!"*
ROMANS 10:15 NIV

Father, thank You for the calling You've placed on my heart to share Your story with others. Although I'm not a professional minister or missionary, I know You have sent me to my own mission field—to the people I am around every day. Help me to see them the way You see them—as beloved children!

ANSWERS TO PRAYER

PRAYER REQUESTS

PRAISES

SATURDAY, SEPTEMBER 6

How beautiful on the mountains are the feet of him who brings good news, who tells of peace and brings good news of happiness, who tells of saving power, and says to Zion, "Your God rules!"
Isaiah 52:7 nlv

Lord, thank You for giving me the privilege of bringing Your encouragement to others. Please show me every opportunity You have for me to promote peace and spread the joy that is knowing that You are in control and Your ways are good.

PRAYER REQUESTS

PRAISES

ANSWERS TO PRAYER

SUNDAY, SEPTEMBER 7

I saw another messenger flying through midheaven. He carried an eternal gospel, bringing good news to all the citizens of the earth—every ethnicity, nation, language, and people.
REVELATION 14:6 VOICE

The message of Jesus Christ is one that will last forever, Lord. The story of Your grace and salvation from Jesus' sacrifice is for everyone—regardless of their education, race, gender, or past. Thank You for not putting stipulations on who can hear and receive the good news. You are an all-welcoming God!

ANSWERS TO PRAYER

PRAYER REQUESTS

PRAISES

MONDAY, SEPTEMBER 8

Then I heard the Lord asking, "Whom should I send as a messenger to this people? Who will go for us?" I said, "Here I am. Send me."
Isaiah 6:8 nlt

Father God, thank You for the people who You have called to minister for a living. I've been blessed by missionaries and pastors and preachers and teachers throughout my faith journey. Help me support them in whatever way I can—through prayer, encouragement, and financial support. Help them see that what they do in Your name makes a difference—now and for eternity.

PRAYER REQUESTS

PRAISES

ANSWERS TO PRAYER

TUESDAY, SEPTEMBER 9

Now, sing to the Eternal, all the earth! Announce the good news of His salvation each and every day!
1 Chronicles 16:23 voice

Your creation displays Your majesty, God! Even unbelievers enjoy the beauty of nature, so help me connect the dots for them between the creation and the Creator. I will talk about the beauty of Your creative hand in a beautiful sunset or a field of wildflowers. Let me plant seeds for Your harvest in the hearts of people around me, even through everyday occurrences.

ANSWERS TO PRAYER

PRAYER REQUESTS

PRAISES

WEDNESDAY, SEPTEMBER 10

Publish his glorious deeds among the nations.
Tell everyone about the amazing things he does.
Psalm 96:3 nlt

When I'm paying attention, Father, I see evidence of Your goodness in my life every day. It's only when I'm distracted by my own selfishness and worries that I don't see Your work! Today I will find something You're doing and tell someone else about it—in the hope they will begin to understand that Your ways are perfect, Lord.

PRAYER REQUESTS

PRAISES

ANSWERS TO PRAYER

THURSDAY, SEPTEMBER 11

"And the Good News about the Kingdom will be preached throughout the whole world, so that all nations will hear it; and then the end will come."

MATTHEW 24:14 NLT

We don't know exactly when You'll return, Jesus—but the Bible tells us it'll be after the gospel has been preached to the entire world. I'm grateful for the people who are actively working to make this happen. You want everyone to accept Your gift of salvation and eternal life. Thank You for making a way!

ANSWERS TO PRAYER

PRAYER REQUESTS

PRAISES

FRIDAY, SEPTEMBER 12

*Again Jesus said, "Peace be with you!
As the Father has sent me, I am sending you."*
JOHN 20:21 NIV

Jesus, it's amazing to think that in the same way God sent You to earth, You send Your followers out with the same goal in mind: to share God's love and add as many people as possible to God's kingdom! Please give me wisdom to see the people You've put in my life who need to hear Your good news.

PRAYER REQUESTS

PRAISES

ANSWERS TO PRAYER

SATURDAY, SEPTEMBER 13

One day as these men were worshiping the Lord and fasting, the Holy Spirit said, "Appoint Barnabas and Saul for the special work to which I have called them." So after more fasting and prayer, the men laid their hands on them and sent them on their way.

Acts 13:2–3 nlt

Holy Spirit, I'm grateful that You have anointed people to make their living by sharing the gospel. These ministers encourage me in my faith and help me to learn how to minister to others.

ANSWERS TO PRAYER

PRAYER REQUESTS

PRAISES

SUNDAY, SEPTEMBER 14

A wide door has been opened to me here to preach the Good News. But there are many who work against me.
1 Corinthians 16:9 nlv

Lord, today I pray for ministers and missionaries who are doing Your work despite hostility and dangerous situations. Keep them safe, Father. Give them courage and boldness and wisdom to continue to preach the gospel. And if they are discouraged by their circumstances, give them a supernatural dose of Your encouragement to continue in their essential work.

PRAYER REQUESTS

PRAISES

ANSWERS TO PRAYER

MONDAY, SEPTEMBER 15

When he saw the crowds, he had compassion for them, because they were harassed and helpless, like sheep without a shepherd.
MATTHEW 9:36 ESV

Jesus, You are my ultimate Shepherd, but You have appointed so many godly people to help shepherd others in Your love here on earth. I am grateful to belong to a flock with such good and faithful leaders. Thank You for the individuals who have cared for me in my faith journey—wise individuals who have shown me Your love in tangible ways.

ANSWERS TO PRAYER

PRAYER REQUESTS

PRAISES

TUESDAY, SEPTEMBER 16

The Lord isn't really being slow about his promise, as some people think. No, he is being patient for your sake. He does not want anyone to be destroyed, but wants everyone to repent.

2 Peter 3:9 NLT

I praise You for Your patience, Lord. Although I long for the day when Jesus returns to earth, I know that His timing is perfect—and He isn't by any means late. Between now and when You return, use me to bring as many people as possible into Your family.

PRAYER REQUESTS

PRAISES

ANSWERS TO PRAYER

WEDNESDAY, SEPTEMBER 17

These were his instructions to them: "The harvest is great, but the workers are few. So pray to the Lord who is in charge of the harvest; ask him to send more workers into his fields."

Luke 10:2 NLT

Father, please raise up the next generation of harvest workers to continue the work Jesus started when He walked on earth. Every moment brings us closer to the Son's return, and we want to be diligent and focused in bringing more and more people into Your kingdom.

ANSWERS TO PRAYER

PRAYER REQUESTS

PRAISES

THURSDAY, SEPTEMBER 18

The Lord replied, "Don't say, 'I'm too young,' for you must go wherever I send you and say whatever I tell you. And don't be afraid of the people, for I will be with you and will protect you. I, the Lord, have spoken!"

JEREMIAH 1:7–8 NLT

Lord, when I feel ill-equipped to represent You, remind me of the great people of faith in the Bible who also felt inadequate. Because the truth is, if You call me to share Your love with someone, You will give me the confidence and ability to do it well!

PRAYER REQUESTS

PRAISES

ANSWERS TO PRAYER

FRIDAY, SEPTEMBER 19

You have heard me teach things that have been confirmed by many reliable witnesses. Now teach these truths to other trustworthy people who will be able to pass them on to others.

2 Timothy 2:2 nlt

Father, although You may not have called me to teach for a living, You have called me to be a teacher in Your kingdom by telling others what You have done in my life. It's a subject matter I know well, so give me the passion to share it boldly.

ANSWERS TO PRAYER

PRAYER REQUESTS

PRAISES

SATURDAY, SEPTEMBER 20

May we never tire of doing what is good and right before our Lord because in His season we shall bring in a great harvest if we can just persist.
GALATIANS 6:9 VOICE

Being a harvester in Your kingdom is a job of endurance, Lord. The good work of sharing the good news is rewarding, but there are times when it feels like nobody is listening. Remind me that whatever I do in Your name is planting seeds of faith that may someday take root and grow!

PRAYER REQUESTS

PRAISES

ANSWERS TO PRAYER

SUNDAY, SEPTEMBER 21

Do your best to know that God is pleased with you. Be as a workman who has nothing to be ashamed of. Teach the words of truth in the right way.
2 Timothy 2:15 nlv

God, You have always given me Your best, and so I want to give my very best effort as I work to expand Your kingdom. Let love and truth guide everything I do, and please bless me with joy in the details of the ministry You have for me.

ANSWERS TO PRAYER

PRAYER REQUESTS

PRAISES

MONDAY, SEPTEMBER 22
First Day of Autumn

"The Son of Man came to seek and to save the lost."
Luke 19:10 NIV

You do more than just offer grace, Jesus. You seek out every lost person because they are *that* important to You. Give me eyes to see the precious treasures that are the people in my life who still need You. Give me the endurance to shine Your light and love on them so that they learn You are here and You never leave.

PRAYER REQUESTS

PRAISES

ANSWERS TO PRAYER

TUESDAY, SEPTEMBER 23

For I am not the least bit embarrassed about the gospel. I won't shy away from it, because it is God's power to save every person who believes.
ROMANS 1:16 VOICE

God, help me to stand strong when Satan tries to convince me that Your message isn't relevant today—that it's old-fashioned and out of step with the times. The truth is that I have been transformed by the power of Your Word and I know the life-saving ability it has for all who believe!

ANSWERS TO PRAYER

PRAYER REQUESTS

PRAISES

WEDNESDAY, SEPTEMBER 24

Pure and genuine religion in the sight of God the Father means caring for orphans and widows in their distress and refusing to let the world corrupt you.
JAMES 1:27 NLT

Give me a tender heart toward the people who have the biggest need of You as their heavenly Father, Lord. You care deeply about the women who have lost husbands and the children who have lost parents, and I do too. Give me opportunities to love and help in Your name.

PRAYER REQUESTS

ANSWERS TO PRAYER

PRAISES

THURSDAY, SEPTEMBER 25

In your hearts revere Christ as Lord. Always be prepared to give an answer to everyone who asks you to give the reason for the hope that you have. But do this with gentleness and respect.
1 Peter 3:15 niv

I want to be ready to engage in meaningful conversation when someone wants to talk about You, Lord. Prepare my heart and help me to organize my thoughts to be able to speak wisely and share Your message without hesitation. My life is full of hope because of You!

ANSWERS TO PRAYER

PRAYER REQUESTS

PRAISES

FRIDAY, SEPTEMBER 26

All of Scripture is God-breathed; in its inspired voice, we hear useful teaching, rebuke, correction, instruction, and training for a life that is right.

2 Timothy 3:16 voice

Lord, I love Your Word. I love the encouragement it brings. I love the stories of Your people. I even love the challenges it sets before me—because I know You are always there through it all. Help me be faithful in reading the Bible and let it have an impact on my thoughts, words, and actions.

PRAYER REQUESTS

PRAISES

ANSWERS TO PRAYER

SATURDAY, SEPTEMBER 27

"Yes, I am the vine; you are the branches. Those who remain in me, and I in them, will produce much fruit. For apart from me you can do nothing."
JOHN 15:5 NLT

I will design my life in a way that I stay firmly rooted to You, Jesus. I will prioritize daily quiet time in Your Word, weekly fellowship with other believers, and moment-by-moment conversations with You in prayer. Please bless my efforts and let my faith flourish!

ANSWERS TO PRAYER

PRAYER REQUESTS

PRAISES

SUNDAY, SEPTEMBER 28

Remember to do good and help each other. Gifts like this please God.
HEBREWS 13:16 NLV

Oh, how I long to please You, God! And when Your Word tells me exactly how to please You, I will pay attention. "Do good and help each other"—what simple instructions! Kind, selfless assistance to others is something that I find pleasure in as well! Today, Lord, show me the good You want me to do. Let me be Your hands and feet to the people around me.

PRAYER REQUESTS

ANSWERS TO PRAYER

PRAISES

MONDAY, SEPTEMBER 29

I planted the seed. Apollos watered it, but it was God Who kept it growing. This shows that the one who plants or the one who waters is not the important one. God is the important One. He makes it grow.
1 Corinthians 3:6–7 nlv

I will faithfully share Your message, Lord. I know that anything I do in Your name can plant faith seeds in the heart of others. I will continue to do the work of sowing seeds, knowing that You are the one who makes those seeds grow, Father.

ANSWERS TO PRAYER

PRAYER REQUESTS

PRAISES

TUESDAY, SEPTEMBER 30

"But his father said to the servants, 'Quick! Bring the finest robe in the house and put it on him. . . . And kill the calf we have been fattening. We must celebrate. . .for this son of mine was dead and has now returned to life. He was lost, but now he is found.' So the party began."

Luke 15:22–24 nlt

Jesus, I will be faithful to pray for and love the people in my life who have walked away from You, and I will celebrate their return!

PRAYER REQUESTS

PRAISES

ANSWERS TO PRAYER

OCTOBER
Changes/Seasons of Life

For everything there is a season, a time for every activity under heaven.
ECCLESIASTES 3:1 NLT

SUNDAY	MONDAY	TUESDAY	WEDNESDAY	THURSDAY	FRIDAY	SATURDAY
			1	2	3	4
5	6	7	8	9	10	11
12	13 Columbus Day	14	15	16	17	18
19	20	21	22	23	24	25
26	27	28	29	30	31 Halloween	

Change is inevitable, unavoidable, no matter how much we long for some things to stay the same. Thankfully, through it all, Jesus Christ is the same yesterday, today, and forever (Hebrews 13:8). He is our solid foundation, the one true constant we can depend on. Whether we eagerly welcome new seasons of life or not, He can help us find purpose and joy in them.

WEDNESDAY, OCTOBER 1

The Lord said to Moses, "Say to Aaron and his sons, 'This is the way you should bring good to the people of Israel. Say to them, "May the Lord bring good to you and keep you. May the Lord make His face shine upon you, and be kind to you. May the Lord show favor toward you, and give you peace." ' "

NUMBERS 6:22–26 NLV

Lord, in whatever season I'm going through or my loved ones are going through, let Your face shine on us.

PRAYER REQUESTS

PRAISES

ANSWERS TO PRAYER

THURSDAY, OCTOBER 2

We know that we belong to God, but the whole world is under the power of the devil. We know God's Son has come. He has given us the understanding to know Him Who is the true God. We are joined together with the true God through His Son, Jesus Christ.
1 John 5:19–20 nlv

I don't understand this painful season I'm in, Lord. It seems so wrong and unfair. Please give me extra love and wisdom and endurance right now. I trust that with Jesus as my Savior, no matter what happens to me, You give me life that lasts forever.

ANSWERS TO PRAYER

PRAYER REQUESTS

PRAISES

FRIDAY, OCTOBER 3

We know that God makes all things work together for the good of those who love Him and are chosen to be a part of His plan.
Romans 8:28 nlv

Father God, help me not to forget that everything really will be okay. Sometimes I can't see how that possibly will happen. But since Your Word promises that You are working all things together for the good of those who love You and have been chosen to be part of Your plan, I believe it.

PRAYER REQUESTS

PRAISES

ANSWERS TO PRAYER

SATURDAY, OCTOBER 4

The Lord brings the plans of nations to nothing. He wrecks the plans of the people. The plans of the Lord stand forever. The plans of His heart stand through the future of all people.
Psalm 33:10–11 nlv

I feel like my plans are wrecked too sometimes. But if they needed to be wrecked, then I trust You, Lord. Show me what Your perfect plans are instead, and please help me to follow them.

ANSWERS TO PRAYER

PRAYER REQUESTS

PRAISES

SUNDAY, OCTOBER 5

Worship Christ as Lord of your life. And if someone asks about your hope as a believer, always be ready to explain it. But do this in a gentle and respectful way. Keep your conscience clear. Then if people speak against you, they will be ashamed when they see what a good life you live because you belong to Christ.

1 Peter 3:15–16 NLT

In whatever season of life I'm in, there are always opportunities to share Your truth and love, Jesus. I want to be ready.

PRAYER REQUESTS

PRAISES

ANSWERS TO PRAYER

MONDAY, OCTOBER 6

There is wonderful joy ahead, even though you must endure many trials for a little while. These trials will show that your faith is genuine. It is being tested as fire tests and purifies gold—though your faith is far more precious than mere gold.
1 Peter 1:6–7 nlt

Lord, help me to remember that hard times prove whether I truly love and believe in You. I want to show You and everyone around me that my faith in You is real and strong!

ANSWERS TO PRAYER

PRAYER REQUESTS

PRAISES

TUESDAY, OCTOBER 7

Anxiety in a man's heart weighs him down, but a good word makes him glad.
PROVERBS 12:25 ESV

Anxiety in my heart sure is weighing me down in this season of change, Lord, so please lift me up with good words. Speak to my heart and mind. Lead me to the scriptures I especially need right now. Help my family and friends say the things You want me to hear to encourage me. Thank You for showing me Your love and care in these ways.

PRAYER REQUESTS

PRAISES

ANSWERS TO PRAYER

WEDNESDAY, OCTOBER 8

I will praise the Lord, who counsels me; even at night my heart instructs me.
I keep my eyes always on the Lord. With him at my right hand, I will not be shaken.
Therefore my heart is glad and my tongue rejoices; my body also will rest secure.
Psalm 16:7–9 niv

Lord, I want to look for all the joy that can come with new changes and seasons in life. Please help me to see life as a journey and adventure with You guiding me through all the highs and lows.

ANSWERS TO PRAYER

PRAYER REQUESTS

PRAISES

THURSDAY, OCTOBER 9

With the Lord one day is as a thousand years, and a thousand years as one day. The Lord is not slow to fulfill his promise as some count slowness, but is patient toward you, not wishing that any should perish, but that all should reach repentance. But the day of the Lord will come like a thief.

2 Peter 3:8–10 esv

Remind me that how I view time is not how You view time, Lord. Your schedule is perfect and is motivated by great love for all people. Day by day, just show me the good things You want me to do as I continue to hope in You.

PRAYER REQUESTS

ANSWERS TO PRAYER

PRAISES

FRIDAY, OCTOBER 10

Give your burdens to the Lord, and he will take care of you. He will not permit the godly to slip and fall.
Psalm 55:22 NLT

Jesus, please help me to just be able to relax and go with the flow more. Life is full of change, and I need to fully accept that reality. I don't want to fear and fight change so much. Help me to find the fun and blessings in it instead.

ANSWERS TO PRAYER

PRAYER REQUESTS

PRAISES

SATURDAY, OCTOBER 11

"God is not a man, so he does not lie. He is not human, so he does not change his mind. Has he ever spoken and failed to act? Has he ever promised and not carried it through?"

Numbers 23:19 nlt

Father God, I'm thankful that You keep Your promises. I trust that You don't act like people who change their minds a lot and even lie to me. You are always dependable. What You say You'll do, You do. What You have spoken, You fulfill.

PRAYER REQUESTS

PRAISES

ANSWERS TO PRAYER

SUNDAY, OCTOBER 12

We rejoice in our sufferings, knowing that suffering produces endurance, and endurance produces character, and character produces hope, and hope does not put us to shame, because God's love has been poured into our hearts through the Holy Spirit who has been given to us.

Romans 5:3–5 esv

Seasons of loss and disappointment will surely find me in this broken world. But You want me to rejoice anyway, and I want to obey You, Lord. Help me to focus on how You are developing endurance, character, and hope in me in the midst of trials.

ANSWERS TO PRAYER

PRAYER REQUESTS

PRAISES

MONDAY, OCTOBER 13
Columbus Day

Wait patiently for the Lord. Be brave and courageous. Yes, wait patiently for the Lord.
Psalm 27:14 nlt

Some seasons feel like nothing but waiting, Lord. Help me to be content with that. Please forgive me when I act impatient and whiny. I want to replace my frustration with praise. I don't know all the things You are doing behind the scenes in my life, but I trust Your plans and Your will for my life.

PRAYER REQUESTS

PRAISES

ANSWERS TO PRAYER

TUESDAY, OCTOBER 14

Nothing can ever separate us from God's love.
ROMANS 8:38 NLT

Father, sometimes I obsess over a big decision because I'm afraid of change and want to know specifically what Your will is for my life. But maybe You want to tell me that, as long as my choice is not disobeying Your Word, I don't have to get so anxious about it. Sometimes there is no "perfect" choice. Please give me peace. Remind me that whatever I decide, nothing can ever separate me from Your love.

ANSWERS TO PRAYER

PRAYER REQUESTS

PRAISES

WEDNESDAY, OCTOBER 15

"Long ago you laid the foundation of the earth and made the heavens with your hands. They will perish, but you remain forever; they will wear out like old clothing. You will change them like a garment and discard them. But you are always the same; you will live forever. The children of your people will live in security. Their children's children will thrive in your presence."
Psalm 102:25–28 nlt

Almighty God, You have always been and always will be. You are my constant peace and hope through every season of life.

PRAYER REQUESTS

ANSWERS TO PRAYER

PRAISES

THURSDAY, OCTOBER 16

"Bring all the tithes into the storehouse so there will be enough food in my Temple. If you do," says the Lord of Heaven's Armies, "I will open the windows of heaven for you. I will pour out a blessing so great you won't have enough room to take it in! Try it! Put me to the test!"

Malachi 3:10 nlt

Even when I'm in a season of strained finances, I want to keep being generous and give to You, Lord. I trust in Your promises and provision.

ANSWERS TO PRAYER

PRAYER REQUESTS

PRAISES

FRIDAY, OCTOBER 17

Since we are surrounded by so great a cloud of witnesses, let us also lay aside every weight, and sin which clings so closely, and let us run with endurance the race that is set before us, looking to Jesus, the founder and perfecter of our faith.

HEBREWS 12:1–2 ESV

Lord, if I find myself in a season that makes me feel disappointed and sad, missing the things that once were, please lift my head. You have set the right path and race before me in Your holy plan for me. I will look to You and keep moving forward.

PRAYER REQUESTS

PRAISES

ANSWERS TO PRAYER

SATURDAY, OCTOBER 18

Where can I go from Your Spirit? Or where can I run away from where You are? If I go up to heaven, You are there! . . . If I take the wings of the morning or live in the farthest part of the sea, even there Your hand will lead me and Your right hand will hold me.
Psalm 139:7–10 nlv

In any season, I am never alone. You, Lord, are with me in every time and place and situation through Your Holy Spirit. Thank You for Your comforting and powerful presence in my life.

ANSWERS TO PRAYER

PRAYER REQUESTS

PRAISES

SUNDAY, OCTOBER 19

*Trust in the Lord with all your heart and lean not on your own understanding;
in all your ways submit to him, and he will make your paths straight.
Do not be wise in your own eyes; fear the Lord and shun evil. This
will bring health to your body and nourishment to your bones.*

Proverbs 3:5–8 niv

I sure can't lean on my own understanding right now, Lord, because I'm so confused by this season of life I'm in. I submit to You. Please guide me out of this mess onto straight paths.

PRAYER REQUESTS

PRAISES

ANSWERS TO PRAYER

MONDAY, OCTOBER 20

Godliness with contentment is great gain, for we brought nothing into the world, and we cannot take anything out of the world. But if we have food and clothing, with these we will be content. But those who desire to be rich fall into temptation, into a snare, into many senseless and harmful desires that plunge people into ruin and destruction. For the love of money is a root of all kinds of evils.

1 Timothy 6:6–10 esv

I don't ever want to be fixated on possessions and wealth, Lord. Seasons of prosperity may come and go, but You alone will ultimately always provide everything I need.

ANSWERS TO PRAYER

PRAYER REQUESTS

PRAISES

TUESDAY, OCTOBER 21

Even my best friend, the one I trusted completely, the one who shared my food, has turned against me. Lord, have mercy on me.
Psalm 41:9–10 NLT

The psalmist prayed about betrayal by a close friend, and I am praying about that too today, God! I feel so lost and so hurt and so angry! Please help me to have self-control and wisdom. Help me to trust that You are working to bring justice to this situation according to Your perfect timing.

PRAYER REQUESTS

ANSWERS TO PRAYER

PRAISES

WEDNESDAY, OCTOBER 22

Since, then, you have been raised with Christ, set your hearts on things above, where Christ is, seated at the right hand of God. Set your minds on things above, not on earthly things. For you died, and your life is now hidden with Christ in God. When Christ, who is your life, appears, then you also will appear with him in glory.
Colossians 3:1–4 niv

Help me to look above it all, Lord, no matter what changes in life I'm going through. I can get through anything when I'm focusing on You for my help and strength.

ANSWERS TO PRAYER

PRAYER REQUESTS

PRAISES

THURSDAY, OCTOBER 23

"O God my rock," I cry, "Why have you forgotten me? Why must I wander around in grief, oppressed by my enemies?" Their taunts break my bones. They scoff, "Where is this God of yours?" Why am I discouraged? Why is my heart so sad? I will put my hope in God! I will praise him again—my Savior and my God!

PSALM 42:9–11 NLT

Even though I do have questions and anguish and discouragement, Lord, I will put my hope in You and choose to praise You, my Savior and my God.

PRAYER REQUESTS

ANSWERS TO PRAYER

PRAISES

FRIDAY, OCTOBER 24

If you are insulted because you bear the name of Christ, you will be blessed, for the glorious Spirit of God rests upon you. If you suffer, however, it must not be for murder, stealing, making trouble, or prying into other people's affairs. But it is no shame to suffer for being a Christian. Praise God for the privilege of being called by his name!

1 Peter 4:14–16 NLT

I feel like I'm in a season of suffering for being a Christian, Lord. Please encourage me with Your promises. Help me to remember what a privilege it is to be called by Your name.

ANSWERS TO PRAYER

PRAYER REQUESTS

PRAISES

SATURDAY, OCTOBER 25

"For I know the plans I have for you, declares the Lord, plans for welfare and not for evil, to give you a future and a hope."
Jeremiah 29:11 esv

Heavenly Father, it's just been feeling like too much lately—all this change. I can't seem to catch my breath from one life-altering event, and then another one happens. Keep me steady and stable as I depend on You. I trust in Your promises that You have good plans for Your people.

PRAYER REQUESTS

PRAISES

ANSWERS TO PRAYER

SUNDAY, OCTOBER 26

"For as the heavens are higher than the earth, so are My ways higher than your ways, and My thoughts than your thoughts."

ISAIAH 55:9 NLV

Lord, You see the bigger picture, and I cannot right now. I want to jump ahead and see the final results and the happy ending of this season, but You are leading me step by step and day by day. Help me to be content with that. Show me and help me appreciate the ways You are growing my faith in You and making me more dependent on You.

ANSWERS TO PRAYER

PRAYER REQUESTS

PRAISES

MONDAY, OCTOBER 27

"Wisdom and power belong to Him. He changes the times and the years. He takes kings away, and puts kings in power. He gives wisdom to wise men and much learning to men of understanding. He makes known secret and hidden things. He knows what is in the darkness. Light is with Him."

Daniel 2:20–22 nlv

Almighty God, when changes that are happening in the world seem scary, remind me that You are always sovereign and in control above them all. I can't possibly see all that You can. I trust You and am grateful to be under Your protection.

PRAYER REQUESTS

ANSWERS TO PRAYER

PRAISES

TUESDAY, OCTOBER 28

If we claim we have no sin, we are only fooling ourselves and not living in the truth. But if we confess our sins to him, he is faithful and just to forgive us our sins and to cleanse us from all wickedness.

1 John 1:8–9 NLT

Lord, I put myself in a terrible season of life because of the sin I chose. I'm so sorry. I'm now admitting my sin and asking You for forgiveness. I'm so grateful for Your mercy and grace that cleanse me and bring me into a new season of walking closely with You again.

ANSWERS TO PRAYER

PRAYER REQUESTS

PRAISES

WEDNESDAY, OCTOBER 29

Get all the advice and instruction you can, so you will be wise the rest of your life. You can make many plans, but the Lord's purpose will prevail.
Proverbs 19:20–21 nlt

God, I feel You leading me into something new. Please give me direction and clarity. Speak boldly into my life regarding this big decision. Lead me to the scriptures and messages You want me to hear. Let wise loved ones in my life give me good insight. I want to listen to advice and accept instruction so that I can gain wisdom.

PRAYER REQUESTS

ANSWERS TO PRAYER

PRAISES

THURSDAY, OCTOBER 30

A joyful heart is good medicine, but a crushed spirit dries up the bones.
PROVERBS 17:22 ESV

God, I believe that, even when I'm struggling in a hard season of life, I can do my best to keep my heart full of joy. Please fill me up with gratitude as I count and focus on all my blessings. Help me to have a good sense of humor and notice many, many reasons to smile and laugh.

ANSWERS TO PRAYER

PRAYER REQUESTS

PRAISES

FRIDAY, OCTOBER 31
Halloween

> *Our citizenship is in heaven, and from it we await a Savior, the Lord Jesus Christ, who will transform our lowly body to be like his glorious body, by the power that enables him even to subject all things to himself.*
>
> Philippians 3:20–21 ESV

Jesus, remind me that every season in this world is just temporary. My final home and my citizenship are with You in heaven. I'm eagerly watching the sky, so excited for the day when You return.

PRAYER REQUESTS

PRAISES

ANSWERS TO PRAYER

NOVEMBER

In Everything Give Thanks

Give thanks to God no matter what circumstances you find yourself in.
1 Thessalonians 5:18 voice

SUNDAY	MONDAY	TUESDAY	WEDNESDAY	THURSDAY	FRIDAY	SATURDAY
						1
2 Daylight Saving Time ends	3	4 Election Day	5	6	7	8
9	10	11 Veterans Day	12	13	14	15
16	17	18	19	20	21	22
23 / 30	24	25	26	27 Thanksgiving	28	29

Is it possible to give thanks in *any* situation? In heartbreak? In death? In failure and disappointment? Through the power of the Holy Spirit, the answer is yes. Sometimes it takes a mental reframing of a difficult situation. Sometimes it takes time, perspective, and encouragement from a godly friend. But we can *choose* to be thankful.

SATURDAY, NOVEMBER 1

This is the day the Lord has made. We will rejoice and be glad in it.
Psalm 118:24 nlt

I woke up this morning, Lord, to a new day with new possibilities. You have made today, and no matter what it brings, I will thank You for air in my lungs, the earth beneath my feet, and another day to live for You. Thank You for going ahead of me and leading the way into today!

PRAYER REQUESTS

PRAISES

ANSWERS TO PRAYER

SUNDAY, NOVEMBER 2
Daylight Saving Time ends

Whatever is good and perfect comes to us from God. He is the One Who made all light. He does not change. No shadow is made by His turning.
James 1:17 nlv

Father, thank You for being a God who doesn't change. You don't waffle or flip-flop or change Your mind or change Your plan. I don't have to wonder what the future holds, because You hold my future in Your hands, and I trust You. You are working all things together for my good.

ANSWERS TO PRAYER

PRAYER REQUESTS

PRAISES

MONDAY, NOVEMBER 3

I have learned to be content in whatever circumstances. I know how to survive in tight situations, and I know how to enjoy having plenty. In fact, I have learned how to face any circumstances: fed or hungry, with or without. I can be content in any and every situation through the Anointed One who is my power and strength.

Philippians 4:11–13 voice

When I'm feeling discontented, Lord, remind me that, no matter what I am facing, I can *choose* to be thankful that You are here with me.

PRAYER REQUESTS

PRAISES

ANSWERS TO PRAYER

TUESDAY, NOVEMBER 4
Election Day

Since we are receiving a Kingdom that is unshakable, let us be thankful and please God by worshiping him with holy fear and awe.
HEBREWS 12:28 NLT

You love me no matter what, Father, and I'm so thankful to be a part of a family that will endure forever. I don't have to worry if the foundation will hold, because Your church is built on Your holy and perfect Son, Jesus. I choose to praise You today!

ANSWERS TO PRAYER

PRAYER REQUESTS

PRAISES

WEDNESDAY, NOVEMBER 5

*Give thanks to the Lord, for He is good,
for His loving-kindness lasts forever.*
Psalm 136:1 nlv

Father, You are good. *Good* doesn't even begin to describe all You are, though! You are holy. You are kind. You are generous. You are patient. You are compassionate and gracious. You are merciful and empathetic. You are powerful and able to do the impossible! All these things are as true today as they were yesterday, and they will remain true forever!

PRAYER REQUESTS

ANSWERS TO PRAYER

PRAISES

THURSDAY, NOVEMBER 6

For the sake of Christ, then, I am content with weaknesses, insults, hardships, persecutions, and calamities. For when I am weak, then I am strong.
2 Corinthians 12:10 esv

Help me to learn to rely on Your strength, Jesus. The world constantly tells me that I should be self-sufficient and not rely on anyone else to take care of me, but Your way is different. I won't be afraid to ask You for help, and when You display Your power, I will tell others of Your greatness!

ANSWERS TO PRAYER

PRAYER REQUESTS

PRAISES

FRIDAY, NOVEMBER 7

*You will keep the peace, a perfect peace, for all who trust in You,
for those who dedicate their hearts and minds to You.*

ISAIAH 26:3 VOICE

Jesus, thank You for the promise of Your peace—Your all-consuming peace that defies understanding. Your peace is a gift that I gladly accept and will embrace every day. I don't have to be anxious and afraid, because I rest in the fact that You will take care of me.

PRAYER REQUESTS

PRAISES

ANSWERS TO PRAYER

SATURDAY, NOVEMBER 8

Enter his gates with thanksgiving and his courts with praise; give thanks to him and praise his name. For the Lord is good and his love endures forever; his faithfulness continues through all generations.

Psalm 100:4–5 niv

Lord, I praise You for who You are. You are my good Father, who loves me. You are faithful to keep Your promises, and You guide me in wisdom and truth. You've always been there for me, and I know that You always will be!

ANSWERS TO PRAYER

PRAYER REQUESTS

PRAISES

SUNDAY, NOVEMBER 9

"Giving thanks is a sacrifice that truly honors me. If you keep to my path, I will reveal to you the salvation of God."

PSALM 50:23 NLT

Some days, being thankful is easy and feels natural. Other days, it feels like hard work. Regardless of how I feel, I will *choose* to live a life of gratitude to You, Lord. I will make it a habit so that *thank You* are the first words I say to You in prayer.

PRAYER REQUESTS

PRAISES

ANSWERS TO PRAYER

MONDAY, NOVEMBER 10

Trust in the Lord with all your heart and lean not on your own understanding; in all your ways submit to him, and he will make your paths straight.

PROVERBS 3:5–6 NIV

God, I trust You! I trust You with the big, monumental things in my life and the small, seemingly insignificant details of my day. Help me to live out that trust in every area. I know You are faithful to lead me well in Your will for my life.

ANSWERS TO PRAYER

PRAYER REQUESTS

PRAISES

TUESDAY, NOVEMBER 11
Veterans Day

*Cast your burden on the Lord, and he will sustain you;
he will never permit the righteous to be moved.*
Psalm 55:22 esv

Lord, thank You for being a God who cares about me personally. Thank You for offering to take my burdens and worries away from me. When I'm able to take the load off my shoulders and give it to You, that's when I feel truly free. That's when grateful praise springs to my lips! Hallelujah!

PRAYER REQUESTS

ANSWERS TO PRAYER

PRAISES

WEDNESDAY, NOVEMBER 12

The Lord is my strength and my safe cover. My heart trusts in Him, and I am helped. So my heart is full of joy. I will thank Him with my song.
Psalm 28:7 nlv

When I feel threatened or in danger, help my heart to trust You more fully, Lord. Because You have helped me in the past, I know that You will help me now and that the fear in my heart will be replaced with songs of joy and thanksgiving.

ANSWERS TO PRAYER

PRAYER REQUESTS

PRAISES

THURSDAY, NOVEMBER 13

God saved you by his grace when you believed. And you can't take credit for this; it is a gift from God.
Ephesians 2:8 nlt

God, You saved me from so much. You saved me from death. You saved me from a debt that I could not pay back. Your grace covers my mistakes—the big and the small—and it gives me hope for the future. I praise You because of the grace that flows from Your very being. I don't deserve it, but I will thank You every day of my life for saving me!

PRAYER REQUESTS

ANSWERS TO PRAYER

PRAISES

FRIDAY, NOVEMBER 14

Don't hold back—give freely, and you'll have plenty poured back into your lap—a good measure, pressed down, shaken together, brimming over. You'll receive in the same measure you give.
LUKE 6:38 VOICE

You love a generous heart, Lord, and I receive great pleasure from giving freely to others. All that would be enough, but You promise to bless me when I give! Thank You for being the perfect example of generosity to follow!

ANSWERS TO PRAYER

PRAYER REQUESTS

PRAISES

SATURDAY, NOVEMBER 15

*"So if you sinful people know how to give good gifts to your children,
how much more will your heavenly Father give good gifts to those who ask him."*

Matthew 7:11 NLT

Lord, thank You for my parents who have sacrificed so much to give good things to their children. You are the perfect Father, God, and I know the gifts You give me will last longer than any earthly gift. Thank You for blessing me yesterday, today, and forever!

PRAYER REQUESTS

PRAISES

ANSWERS TO PRAYER

SUNDAY, NOVEMBER 16

*If you do not have wisdom, ask God for it. He is always ready
to give it to you and will never say you are wrong for asking.*
JAMES 1:5 NLV

When I'm struggling with how to pray in a situation, Lord, remind me that I can ask for Your wisdom. Thank You for always being ready and willing to give me Your insight and a dose of truth to help me navigate hard times, and thank You for never making me feel bad for asking!

ANSWERS TO PRAYER

PRAYER REQUESTS

PRAISES

MONDAY, NOVEMBER 17

Through Jesus, therefore, let us continually offer to God a sacrifice of praise—the fruit of lips that openly profess his name.
Hebrews 13:15 niv

Lord, I praise You today because of Your perfection. I worship You because You are God (and I am not). I am in awe of Your wisdom and limitless power. Thank You for the ways You move in my life every moment of every day and night. You never sleep—You are always working for Your plan to be done!

PRAYER REQUESTS

ANSWERS TO PRAYER

PRAISES

TUESDAY, NOVEMBER 18

You are my God, and I give You thanks; You are my God, and I praise You.
Psalm 118:28 voice

God, You have called me Yours—Your friend, Your treasured daughter, the apple of Your eye. But not only do I belong to You; *You* belong to *me*! You are my God. When my eyes are downcast in the struggle of life, all I have to do is look up and I will see You with Your arms outstretched. We are bound together and belong to each other.

ANSWERS TO PRAYER

PRAYER REQUESTS

PRAISES

WEDNESDAY, NOVEMBER 19

You must keep praying. Keep watching! Be thankful always.
Colossians 4:2 nlv

Lord, I am eagerly waiting and watching for You to act. I absolutely believe that You *are* working—even when I can't see it or feel it. While I wait, I will continue to praise You and pray for Your will to be done. I'm keeping my eyes peeled for the ways You are moving. I trust Your plans in everything, God, and I know they will be done.

PRAYER REQUESTS

ANSWERS TO PRAYER

PRAISES

THURSDAY, NOVEMBER 20

So they took away the stone. And Jesus lifted up his eyes and said, "Father, I thank you that you have heard me."

JOHN 11:41 ESV

Jesus, let me learn from the faith You displayed in bringing Lazarus back to life. When You asked Your Father to display His glory in raising Your friend from the grave, You knew God heard You and was listening intently to Your heart. Father God, thank You for doing the same for me when I pray.

ANSWERS TO PRAYER

PRAYER REQUESTS

PRAISES

FRIDAY, NOVEMBER 21

*Let all that I am praise the Lord; with my whole heart,
I will praise his holy name. Let all that I am praise the Lord;
may I never forget the good things he does for me.*
Psalm 103:1–2 nlt

I don't want to hold back any part of me when I praise You, God! Today I am setting aside the distractions of my to-do list and schedule and worries about tomorrow to focus on one thing: worshipping You for who You are. You are so good to me!

PRAYER REQUESTS

PRAISES

ANSWERS TO PRAYER

SATURDAY, NOVEMBER 22

And now, just as you accepted Christ Jesus as your Lord, you must continue to follow him. Let your roots grow down into him, and let your lives be built on him. Then your faith will grow strong in the truth you were taught, and you will overflow with thankfulness.

Colossians 2:6–7 nlt

I'm rooting down into You, Lord Jesus. I'm digging into scripture and talking to You about everything I'm experiencing. Please help my faith to grow, as I know You will. Thank You!

ANSWERS TO PRAYER

PRAYER REQUESTS

PRAISES

SUNDAY, NOVEMBER 23

I will give thanks to the Lord with all my heart.
I will tell of all the great things You have done.
Psalm 9:1 nlv

When You do great things in my life, Lord, I will tell others about it! Then Your work will not just bless me, but it could encourage someone else as well. Thank You, Father, for the gift it is to live for You. I live with hope. I live with joy. I live anchored to the security that You love me and You are for me.

PRAYER REQUESTS

PRAISES

ANSWERS TO PRAYER

MONDAY, NOVEMBER 24

I will give thanks to the Lord because He is right and good.
I will sing praise to the name of the Lord Most High.
Psalm 7:17 nlv

I have a song on my lips today, God. That song is praise to You! I will join with the birds as they sing in the morning and the sun as it displays Your grandeur as it sets. You are right. You are good. You are holy. You are all the things I want to be. Thank You for welcoming me into Your family.

ANSWERS TO PRAYER

PRAYER REQUESTS

PRAISES

TUESDAY, NOVEMBER 25

Dear brothers and sisters, we can't help but thank God for you, because your faith is flourishing and your love for one another is growing.
2 Thessalonians 1:3 nlt

Father, thank You for the Christian brothers and sisters You've placed in my life. They are such blessings to me, and I know that You use them to speak wisdom into my life. Thank You for surrounding me with like-minded friends so I don't have to go through life alone.

PRAYER REQUESTS

PRAISES

ANSWERS TO PRAYER

WEDNESDAY, NOVEMBER 26

*We give thanks to God always for all of you,
constantly mentioning you in our prayers.*
1 Thessalonians 1:2 esv

When I say I will pray for someone else, Lord, help me be committed to talking to You about them and their situation. I will pray and pray again until You act, Lord! I believe in the power of prayer, so please display Your power even when my prayers are inadequate and ineloquent. Thank You for always hearing me, Father.

ANSWERS TO PRAYER

PRAYER REQUESTS

PRAISES

THURSDAY, NOVEMBER 27
Thanksgiving

*The name of the True God will be my song,
an uplifting tune of praise and thanksgiving!*
Psalm 69:30 voice

I want to live a life of thanksgiving, God—not just today but *every* day! Because the truth is that, even when I don't *feel* thankful, I still have so much to be thankful for. I will not miss the opportunity to tell others about how much You have blessed me in the past, are blessing me today, and will continue to provide for me in the future!

PRAYER REQUESTS

PRAISES

ANSWERS TO PRAYER

FRIDAY, NOVEMBER 28

Don't run from tests and hardships, brothers and sisters. As difficult as they are, you will ultimately find joy in them; if you embrace them, your faith will blossom under pressure and teach you true patience as you endure.

JAMES 1:2–3 VOICE

Lord, in difficult times, I thank You for the promise of this scripture. I need joy and greater faith to result from what I'm dealing with right now. Please give me the strength I need to endure, mature, and grow!

ANSWERS TO PRAYER

PRAYER REQUESTS

PRAISES

SATURDAY, NOVEMBER 29

"The Lord bless you and keep you; the Lord make his face to shine upon you and be gracious to you; the Lord lift up his countenance upon you and give you peace."
Numbers 6:24–26 ESV

Gracious Father and Lord, throughout my life, You've been so faithful to give me good gifts. Your light shines through the daily grace You lavish on me. When I pursue peace, You are faithful to give me a heart at rest. Thank You!

PRAYER REQUESTS

PRAISES

ANSWERS TO PRAYER

SUNDAY, NOVEMBER 30

O my soul, come, praise the Eternal; sing a song from a grateful heart; sing and never forget all the good He has done.
Psalm 103:2 voice

I will never forget the good You bring into my life, Lord. I will constantly remember the ways You have worked in the past. The unexpected blessings You've given me fill me with hope that You will work in amazing ways again! Today I am celebrating Your goodness with a grateful heart. Thank You, thank You, Father!

ANSWERS TO PRAYER

PRAYER REQUESTS

PRAISES

DECEMBER
God's Good Gifts

Every good gift and every perfect gift is from above, coming down from the Father of lights, with whom there is no variation or shadow due to change.
JAMES 1:17 ESV

SUNDAY	MONDAY	TUESDAY	WEDNESDAY	THURSDAY	FRIDAY	SATURDAY
	1	2	3	4	5	6
7	8	9	10	11	12	13
14 Hanukkah begins at Sundown	15	16	17	18	19	20
21 First Day of Winter	22	23	24 Christmas Eve	25 Christmas Day	26	27
28	29	30	31 New Year's Eve			

Every good thing we ever receive in this life ultimately comes from our Father in heaven, who loves us so dearly and bestows gifts even better than the very best earthly parent (Luke 11:11–13). We should enjoy our blessings and also share them generously, with gratitude and praise to the giver of life and breath and everything else (Acts 17:25).

MONDAY, DECEMBER 1

*When sin had power over your life, you were not right with God. . . .
But now you are free from the power of sin. You have become a servant
for God. Your life is set apart for God-like living. The end is life that lasts
forever. You get what is coming to you when you sin. It is death! But God's
free gift is life that lasts forever. It is given to us by our Lord Jesus Christ.*
ROMANS 6:20, 22–23 NLV

The greatest gift of all is the salvation and eternal life that only You can give, Jesus! Thank You for offering it to all people!

ANSWERS TO PRAYER

PRAYER REQUESTS

PRAISES

TUESDAY, DECEMBER 2

God saved you by his grace when you believed. And you can't take credit for this; it is a gift from God. Salvation is not a reward for the good things we have done, so none of us can boast about it.

Ephesians 2:8–9 nlt

You give the gift of salvation based on nothing other than Your great love for us. There is nothing we do to earn it—no works that must be done or checklist to complete first. You are a generous, merciful, loving Father who wants to give salvation from sin and eternal life to everyone who truly believes in You. Hallelujah!

PRAYER REQUESTS

PRAISES

ANSWERS TO PRAYER

WEDNESDAY, DECEMBER 3

Those who won't care for their relatives, especially those in their own household, have denied the true faith. Such people are worse than unbelievers.
1 Timothy 5:8 nlt

I'm grateful for the gift of family, Lord! Remind me how important it is that we take good care of each other. Though we will have conflict at times, help us to cultivate love, peace, and joy in our relationships.

ANSWERS TO PRAYER

PRAYER REQUESTS

PRAISES

THURSDAY, DECEMBER 4

Children are a gift from the Lord. The children born to us are our special reward. The children of a young man are like arrows in the hand of a soldier. Happy is the man who has many of them.
Psalm 127:3–5 nlv

Lord, I want the children in my life to know how precious and treasured they are. And mostly, I want them to trust in You as Savior. Please help me to constantly point them to faith in You.

PRAYER REQUESTS

PRAISES

ANSWERS TO PRAYER

FRIDAY, DECEMBER 5

Two people are better off than one, for they can help each other succeed. If one person falls, the other can reach out and help. But someone who falls alone is in real trouble. . . . A person standing alone can be attacked and defeated, but two can stand back-to-back and conquer. Three are even better, for a triple-braided cord is not easily broken.
Ecclesiastes 4:9–10, 12 nlt

The dear friendships in my life are such a treasure, God. Thank You for connecting me with people who encourage and support me and just enjoy spending time with me.

ANSWERS TO PRAYER

PRAYER REQUESTS

PRAISES

SATURDAY, DECEMBER 6

Tell those who are rich in this world not to be proud and not to trust in their money. Money cannot be trusted. They should put their trust in God. He gives us all we need for our happiness. Tell them to do good and be rich in good works. They should give much to those in need and be ready to share.
1 Timothy 6:17–18 nlv

Father, thank You for the gift of money here on earth, but help me not to trust in it or in my own ability to obtain it. I trust in You, the giver of all, to provide for and bless me.

PRAYER REQUESTS

PRAISES

ANSWERS TO PRAYER

SUNDAY, DECEMBER 7

"Sir," the woman said, "you have nothing to draw with and the well is deep. Where can you get this living water?" . . . Jesus answered, "Everyone who drinks this water will be thirsty again, but whoever drinks the water I give them will never thirst. Indeed, the water I give them will become in them a spring of water welling up to eternal life."

John 4:11, 13–14 niv

Jesus, only You can offer the gift of living water welling up to eternal life. Only You can save and satisfy.

ANSWERS TO PRAYER

PRAYER REQUESTS

PRAISES

MONDAY, DECEMBER 8

Not all flesh is the same: People have one kind of flesh, animals have another, birds another and fish another. There are also heavenly bodies and there are earthly bodies; but the splendor of the heavenly bodies is one kind, and the splendor of the earthly bodies is another.

1 Corinthians 15:39–40 niv

The bodies You have designed for us are incredible, God! Thank You for all that I am capable of doing and enjoying with my body through work and sports and recreation. And thank You for the promise of brand-new, heavenly bodies one day that will never wear out.

PRAYER REQUESTS

PRAISES

ANSWERS TO PRAYER

TUESDAY, DECEMBER 9

The Holy Spirit produces this kind of fruit in our lives: love, joy, peace, patience, kindness, goodness, faithfulness, gentleness, and self-control. There is no law against these things!
Galatians 5:22–23 nlt

Lord, as I live in close relationship with You, please help me produce loads of the fruit of Your Spirit in my life—and then help me share it all with others.

ANSWERS TO PRAYER

PRAYER REQUESTS

PRAISES

WEDNESDAY, DECEMBER 10

The LORD has given them special skills as engravers, designers, embroiderers in blue, purple, and scarlet thread on fine linen cloth, and weavers. They excel as craftsmen and as designers.

EXODUS 35:35 NLT

Thank You for the artistry and creative abilities You have given people, Lord. There are so many ways to fill this earth with beauty: visual art, music, craftsmanship, design, theater, cooking, and on and on and on. We are creative because You are the master Creator and You made us in Your image.

PRAYER REQUESTS

PRAISES

ANSWERS TO PRAYER

THURSDAY, DECEMBER 11

Praise be to the God and Father of our Lord Jesus Christ, the Father of compassion and the God of all comfort, who comforts us in all our troubles, so that we can comfort those in any trouble with the comfort we ourselves receive from God. For just as we share abundantly in the sufferings of Christ, so also our comfort abounds through Christ.
2 Corinthians 1:3–5 niv

Thank You for the gifts of both physical comfort and emotional comfort, Father.

ANSWERS TO PRAYER

PRAYER REQUESTS

PRAISES

FRIDAY, DECEMBER 12

God blessed Noah and his sons and told them, "Be fruitful and multiply. Fill the earth. All the animals of the earth, all the birds of the sky, all the small animals that scurry along the ground, and all the fish in the sea will look on you with fear and terror. I have placed them in your power. I have given them to you for food, just as I have given you grain and vegetables.

Genesis 9:1–3 NLT

God, I praise You for every animal and plant that fills our world with beauty and nourishes our bodies! You are an amazing Creator!

PRAYER REQUESTS

ANSWERS TO PRAYER

PRAISES

SATURDAY, DECEMBER 13

"A rich man had a fertile farm that produced fine crops. He said to himself, 'What should I do? I don't have room for all my crops.' Then he said, 'I know! I'll tear down my barns and build bigger ones. Then I'll have room enough to store all my wheat and other goods. . . .' But God said to him, 'You fool! You will die this very night. Then who will get everything you worked for?' Yes, a person is a fool to store up earthly wealth but not have a rich relationship with God."

Luke 12:16–18, 20–21 nlt

Father, remind me that far better than monetary wealth is a rich relationship with You. It's such a gift to be Your child!

ANSWERS TO PRAYER

PRAYER REQUESTS

PRAISES

SUNDAY, DECEMBER 14
Hanukkah begins at Sundown

How joyful are those who fear the Lord—all who follow his ways! You will enjoy the fruit of your labor. How joyful and prosperous you will be! Your wife will be like a fruitful grapevine, flourishing within your home. Your children will be like vigorous young olive trees as they sit around your table. That is the Lord's blessing for those who fear him.
Psalm 128:1–4 NLT

Joy and prosperity are the rewards for living for You, Lord. I trust You now and forever!

PRAYER REQUESTS

PRAISES

ANSWERS TO PRAYER

MONDAY, DECEMBER 15

The Lord is my shepherd, I lack nothing. He makes me lie down in green pastures, he leads me beside quiet waters, he refreshes my soul. He guides me along the right paths for his name's sake. Even though I walk through the darkest valley, I will fear no evil, for you are with me. . . . Surely your goodness and love will follow me all the days of my life, and I will dwell in the house of the Lord forever.

Psalm 23:1-4, 6 niv

Jesus, it's such a gift to be guided by You, my Good Shepherd.

ANSWERS TO PRAYER

PRAYER REQUESTS

PRAISES

TUESDAY, DECEMBER 16

Dear friend, I pray that you may enjoy good health and that all may go well with you, even as your soul is getting along well.

3 John 2 niv

Lord, thank You for times of strength and good health for myself and for my loved ones. During times of sickness and weakness, I pray You restore us quickly. Ultimately, I'm so glad that one day You'll give perfect heavenly bodies to all who trust in You as Savior.

PRAYER REQUESTS

PRAISES

ANSWERS TO PRAYER

WEDNESDAY, DECEMBER 17

We have different gifts, according to the grace given to each of us. If your gift is prophesying, then prophesy in accordance with your faith; if it is serving, then serve; if it is teaching, then teach; if it is to encourage, then give encouragement; if it is giving, then give generously; if it is to lead, do it diligently; if it is to show mercy, do it cheerfully.
Romans 12:6–8 niv

Lord, please help me to realize what spiritual gifts You have given me and which ones are not for me. I want to use mine well to bless others and worship You!

ANSWERS TO PRAYER

PRAYER REQUESTS

PRAISES

THURSDAY, DECEMBER 18

Each of you should use whatever gift you have received to serve others, as faithful stewards of God's grace in its various forms. If anyone speaks, they should do so as one who speaks the very words of God. If anyone serves, they should do so with the strength God provides, so that in all things God may be praised through Jesus Christ.
1 Peter 4:10–11 niv

Lord, remind me that my gifts are never just collectibles. They are meant to be used regularly to serve others and point people to You, giving You all the gratitude and glory!

PRAYER REQUESTS

PRAISES

ANSWERS TO PRAYER

FRIDAY, DECEMBER 19

"Blessed be your glorious name, and may it be exalted above all blessing and praise. You alone are the Lord. You made the heavens, even the highest heavens, and all their starry host, the earth and all that is on it, the seas and all that is in them. You give life to everything, and the multitudes of heaven worship you."

Nehemiah 9:5–6 niv

The world is full of such an incredible variety of landscapes and climates and scenery. I'd love to see every inch of the beautiful earth You created for us, God!

ANSWERS TO PRAYER

PRAYER REQUESTS

PRAISES

SATURDAY, DECEMBER 20

Put out of your life all these things: bad feelings about other people, anger, temper, loud talk, bad talk which hurts other people, and bad feelings which hurt other people. You must be kind to each other. Think of the other person. Forgive other people just as God forgave you because of Christ's death on the cross.

Ephesians 4:31–32 nlv

You have given me so much forgiveness, Lord, so help me to generously offer that gift to others as well.

PRAYER REQUESTS

PRAISES

ANSWERS TO PRAYER

SUNDAY, DECEMBER 21
First Day of Winter

I will bless the Lord at all times. His praise shall continually be in my mouth. My soul shall make its boast in the Lord. The humble shall hear of it and be glad. O magnify the Lord with me, and let us exalt His name together. I sought the Lord, and He heard me and delivered me from all my fears.
PSALM 34:1–4 SKJV

What a gift it is that You listen and care about all my fears and anxiety, Lord. Thank You for delivering me.

ANSWERS TO PRAYER

PRAYER REQUESTS

PRAISES

MONDAY, DECEMBER 22

"Each of you must repent of your sins and turn to God, and be baptized in the name of Jesus Christ for the forgiveness of your sins. Then you will receive the gift of the Holy Spirit. This promise is to you, to your children, and to those far away—all who have been called by the Lord our God."

ACTS 2:38–39 NLT

Lord, thank You for offering the gift of the Holy Spirit. I pray more and more people receive You!

PRAYER REQUESTS

PRAISES

ANSWERS TO PRAYER

TUESDAY, DECEMBER 23

"Keep on asking, and you will receive what you ask for. Keep on seeking, and you will find. Keep on knocking, and the door will be opened to you. For everyone who asks, receives. Everyone who seeks, finds. And to everyone who knocks, the door will be opened."

MATTHEW 7:7–8 NLT

Lord, I'm so grateful I can keep coming to You in prayer. Please bless me according to Your will.

ANSWERS TO PRAYER

PRAYER REQUESTS

PRAISES

WEDNESDAY, DECEMBER 24
Christmas Eve

The disciples came to Jesus, saying, "Who is the greatest in the kingdom of heaven?" And calling to him a child, he put him in the midst of them and said, "Truly, I say to you, unless you turn and become like children, you will never enter the kingdom of heaven. Whoever humbles himself like this child is the greatest in the kingdom of heaven. Whoever receives one such child in my name receives me."

MATTHEW 18:1–5 ESV

What a gift children are, Lord! Thank You for the little ones in my life. Help me to love and guide them well and also to learn from them.

PRAYER REQUESTS

PRAISES

ANSWERS TO PRAYER

THURSDAY, DECEMBER 25
Christmas Day

For to us a child is born, to us a son is given; and the government shall be upon his shoulder, and his name shall be called Wonderful Counselor, Mighty God, Everlasting Father, Prince of Peace.
ISAIAH 9:6 ESV

Father God, I celebrate with gratitude the precious gift of Your one and only Son, Jesus Christ. You sent Him into the world to be our Savior and Messiah, Immanuel, God with us! Hallelujah!

ANSWERS TO PRAYER

PRAYER REQUESTS

PRAISES

FRIDAY, DECEMBER 26

"Give, and you will receive. Your gift will return to you in full—pressed down, shaken together to make room for more, running over, and poured into your lap. The amount you give will determine the amount you get back."

Luke 6:38 NLT

I want to follow Your ways, Lord, even when they're so opposite of what the world says is wise. Remind me that the more I give away, the more gifts from You I will receive.

PRAYER REQUESTS

PRAISES

ANSWERS TO PRAYER

SATURDAY, DECEMBER 27

"Think how the flowers grow. They do not work or make cloth. But I tell you that Solomon in all his greatness was not dressed as well as one of these flowers. God clothes the grass of the field. It lives today and is burned in the stove tomorrow. How much more will He give you clothes?"
Matthew 6:28–30 nlv

Lord, remind me that You give beauty to even the flowers of this world, so You will surely give beautiful things to Your children. Thank You for all that You've already given me and all that You will continue to give.

ANSWERS TO PRAYER

PRAYER REQUESTS

PRAISES

SUNDAY, DECEMBER 28

"Do not set your heart on what you will eat or drink; do not worry about it. For the pagan world runs after all such things, and your Father knows that you need them. But seek his kingdom, and these things will be given to you as well."

Luke 12:29–31 niv

Lord, remind me to never worry about what gifts You give me and when. You will always provide for my needs at just the right time, and You bless me with extras on top. Help me to keep my focus on following You and seeking Your kingdom. Everything else will fall perfectly into place.

PRAYER REQUESTS

PRAISES

ANSWERS TO PRAYER

MONDAY, DECEMBER 29

God has not given us a spirit of fear and timidity, but of power, love, and self-discipline. So never be ashamed to tell others about our Lord.
2 Timothy 1:7–8 nlt

God, I'm grateful for the spirit You've given me. When I'm tempted to fear or quit or hide, remind me that You have given me power and love and self-discipline. I can stand strong and courageous because You are always with me.

ANSWERS TO PRAYER

PRAYER REQUESTS

PRAISES

TUESDAY, DECEMBER 30

Love is patient and kind. Love is not jealous or boastful or proud or rude. It does not demand its own way. It is not irritable, and it keeps no record of being wronged. It does not rejoice about injustice but rejoices whenever the truth wins out. Love never gives up, never loses faith, is always hopeful, and endures through every circumstance. . . . Three things will last forever—faith, hope, and love—and the greatest of these is love.
1 Corinthians 13:4–7, 13 nlt

Love is what You say it is, Lord. Thank You for giving the world the gift of love.

PRAYER REQUESTS

PRAISES

ANSWERS TO PRAYER

WEDNESDAY, DECEMBER 31
New Year's Eve

How great is the goodness you have stored up for those who fear you. You lavish it on those who come to you for protection, blessing them before the watching world. . . . Praise the Lord, for he has shown me the wonders of his unfailing love.
PSALM 31:19, 21 NLT

God, I'm so grateful for Your promise to bless me lavishly with Your goodness, both here on earth now and in heaven someday in the future.

ANSWERS TO PRAYER

PRAYER REQUESTS

PRAISES

NOTES

CONTRIBUTORS

Annie Barkley made up her first story at the ripe old age of two when she asked her mom to write it down for her. Since then she has read and written many words as a student, newspaper reporter, author, and editor. She has a passion for making God's Word come to life for readers through devotions and Bible study. Annie loves snow (which is a good thing because she lives in Ohio), wearing scarves, eating sushi, playing Scrabble, and spending time with friends and family. Annie wrote entries for February, March, May, July, September, and November.

JoAnne Simmons is a writer and editor who's in awe of God's love and the ways He guides and provides. Her favorite things include coffee shops, libraries, the Bible, good grammar, being a wife and mom, dogs, music, punctuation, church, the beach, and many dear family and friends—but not in that order. If her family weren't so loving and flexible, she'd be in big trouble; and if God's mercies weren't new every morning, she'd never get out of bed. JoAnne wrote entries for January, April, June, August, October, and December.